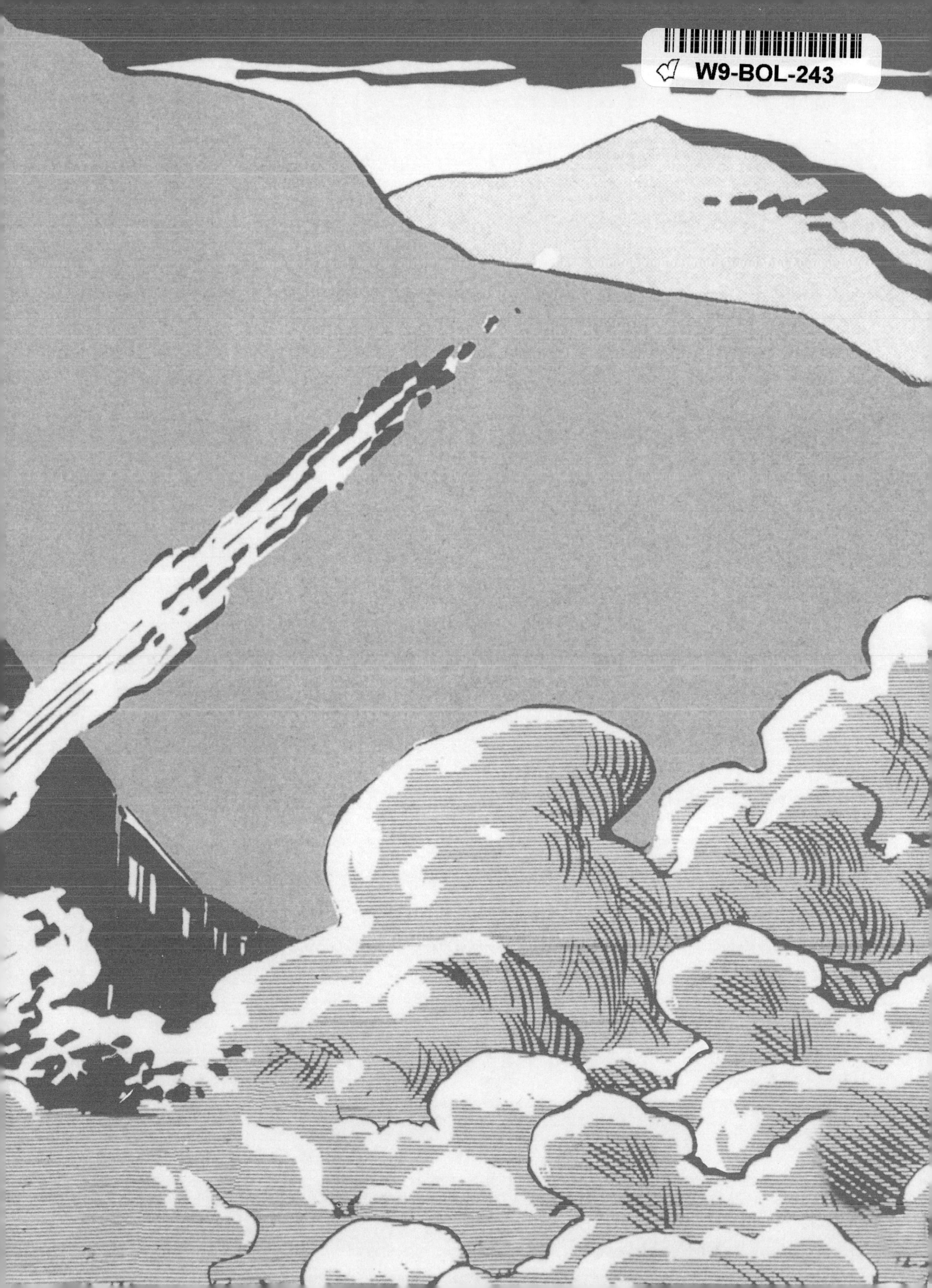

SNOWPIERCER

1: THE ESCAPE

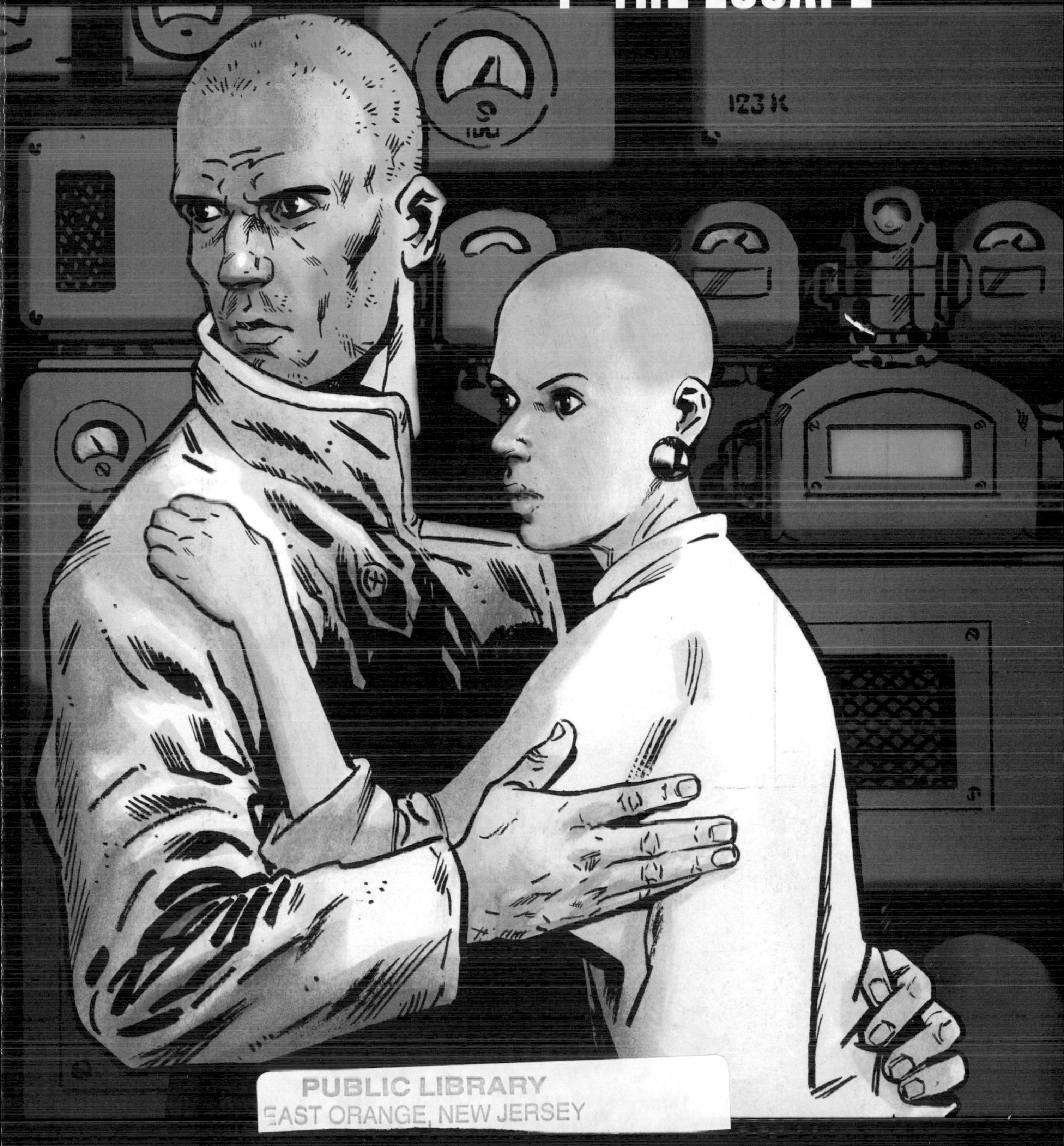
123 K

LOB / ROCHETTE

SNO
v.1

SNOWPIERCER
1: THE ESCAPE

WRITTEN BY

JACQUES LOB

ART BY

JEAN-MARC ROCHETTE

TRANSLATED BY

VIRGINIE SELAVY

LETTERING BY

GABRIELA HOUSTON

What did you think of this book?
We love to hear from our readers.
Please email us at: **readercomments@titanemail.com,**
or write to us at the address opposite.

To receive news, competitions, and exclusive offers online,
please sign up for the Titan Comics newsletter on our website:
www.titan-comics.com

Follow us on Twitter **@ComicsTitan**

Visit us at **facebook.com/comicstitan**

TitanCOMICS

COLLECTION EDITOR
GABRIELA HOUSTON
COLLECTION DESIGNER
SARA GREASLEY

Senior Editor
Steve White
Titan Comics Editorial
Andrew James, Jon Chapple
Production Supervisors
Kelly Fenlon, Jackie Flook
Interim Production Assistant
Peter James
Art Director
Oz Browne
Studio Manager
Selina Juneja
Circulation Manager
Steve Tothill
Marketing Manager
Ricky Claydon
Senior Marketing and Press Executive
Owen Johnson
Marketing Assistant
Tara Felton
Publishing Manager
Darryl Tothill
Publishing Director
Chris Teather
Operations Director
Leigh Baulch
Executive Director
Vivian Cheung
Publisher
Nick Landau

SNOWPIERCER VOLUME 1: THE ESCAPE

HC: 9781782761334
SC: 9781782761389

Published by Titan Comics
A division of Titan Publishing Group Ltd.
144 Southwark St.
London
SE1 0UP

A CIP catalogue record for this title is available
from the British Library.

First edition: February 2014

Originally published in 1984 by
Casterman, France as *Transperceneige*,
and reissued as *Transperceneige: L'Échappé* in 1999.

10 9 8 7 6 5 4 3 2 1

Printed in China.
Titan Comics. TC0234

$ 19.99
1/22/14
8b

i1404T789

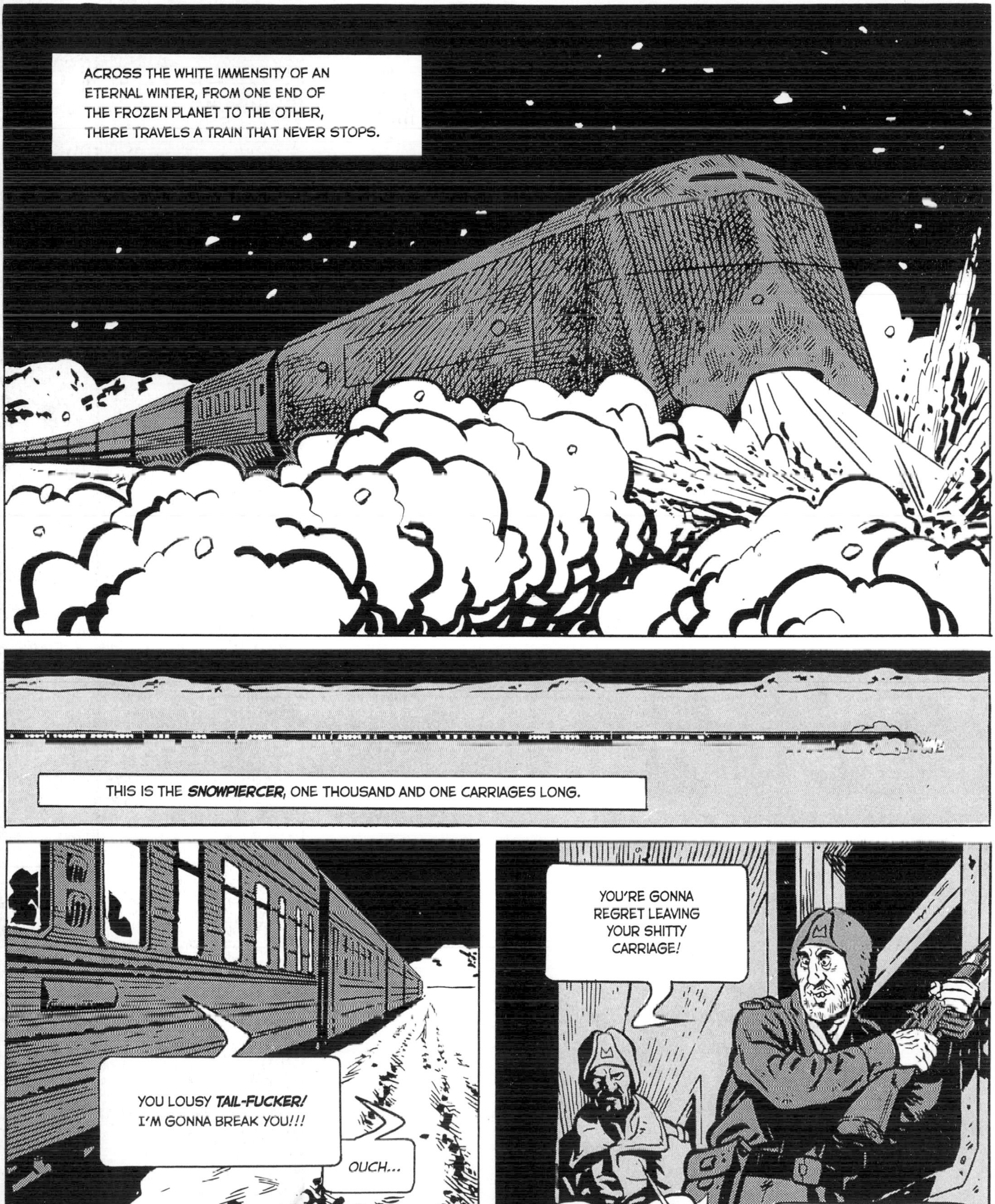

ACROSS THE WHITE IMMENSITY OF AN ETERNAL WINTER, FROM ONE END OF THE FROZEN PLANET TO THE OTHER, THERE TRAVELS A TRAIN THAT NEVER STOPS.
THIS IS THE SNOWPIERCER, ONE THOUSAND AND ONE CARRIAGES LONG.
YOU LOUSY TAIL-FUCKER! I'M GONNA BREAK YOU!!!
OUCH...
THIS IS THE LAST BASTION OF CIVILIZATION...
YOU'RE GONNA REGRET LEAVING YOUR SHITTY CARRIAGE!
TBAP
HEY, EASY! BETTER NOT MESS HIM UP TOO MUCH BEFORE THE CHIEF SEES HIM...

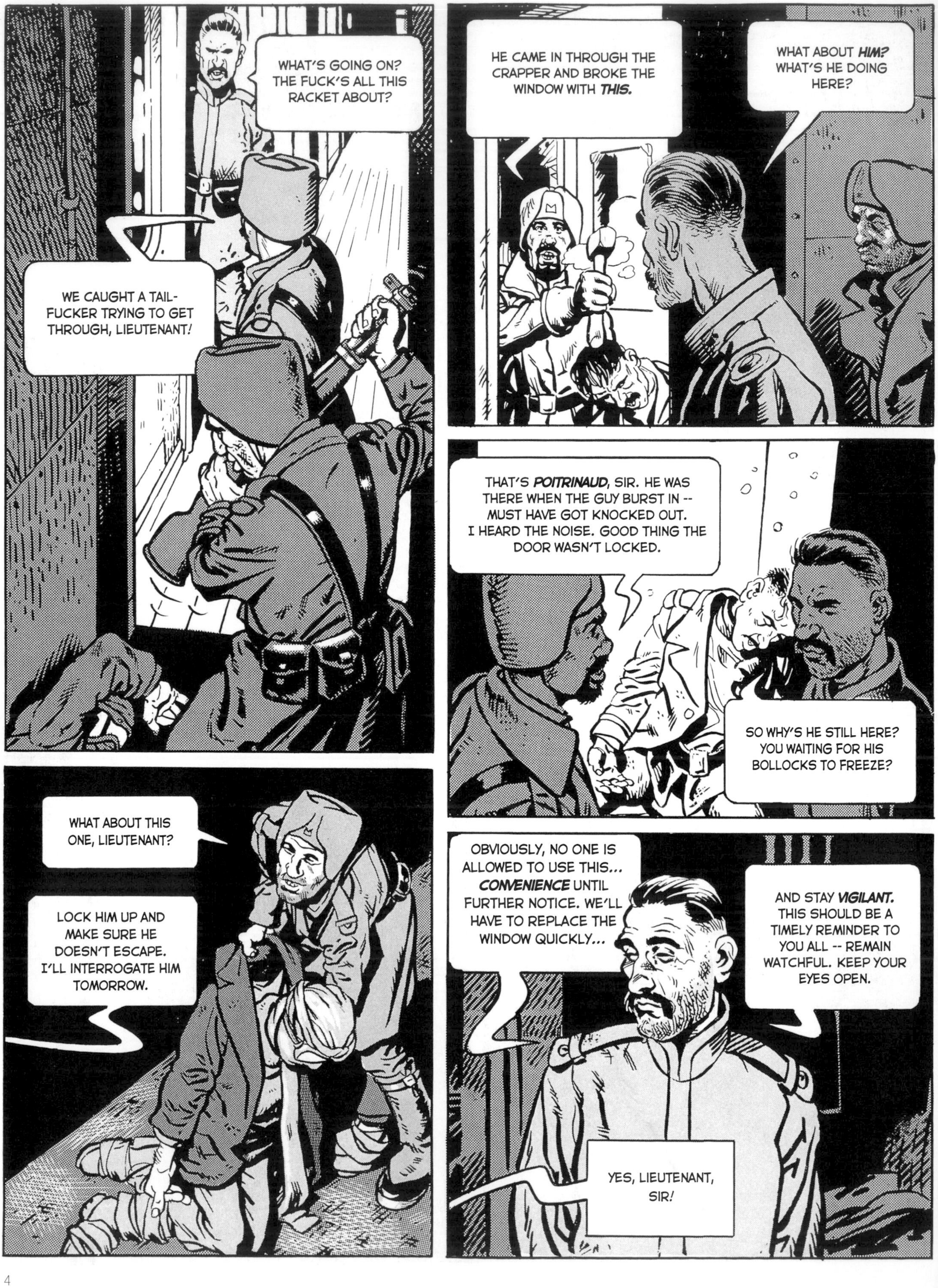
WHAT'S GOING ON? THE FUCK'S ALL THIS RACKET ABOUT?
WE CAUGHT A TAIL-FUCKER TRYING TO GET THROUGH, LIEUTENANT!
HE CAME IN THROUGH THE CRAPPER AND BROKE THE WINDOW WITH ***THIS.***
WHAT ABOUT ***HIM?*** WHAT'S HE DOING HERE?
THAT'S ***POITRINAUD***, SIR. HE WAS THERE WHEN THE GUY BURST IN -- MUST HAVE GOT KNOCKED OUT. I HEARD THE NOISE. GOOD THING THE DOOR WASN'T LOCKED.
SO WHY'S HE STILL HERE? YOU WAITING FOR HIS BOLLOCKS TO FREEZE?
WHAT ABOUT THIS ONE, LIEUTENANT?
LOCK HIM UP AND MAKE SURE HE DOESN'T ESCAPE. I'LL INTERROGATE HIM TOMORROW.
OBVIOUSLY, NO ONE IS ALLOWED TO USE THIS... ***CONVENIENCE*** UNTIL FURTHER NOTICE. WE'LL HAVE TO REPLACE THE WINDOW QUICKLY...
AND STAY ***VIGILANT.*** THIS SHOULD BE A TIMELY REMINDER TO YOU ALL -- REMAIN WATCHFUL. KEEP YOUR EYES OPEN.
YES, LIEUTENANT, SIR!

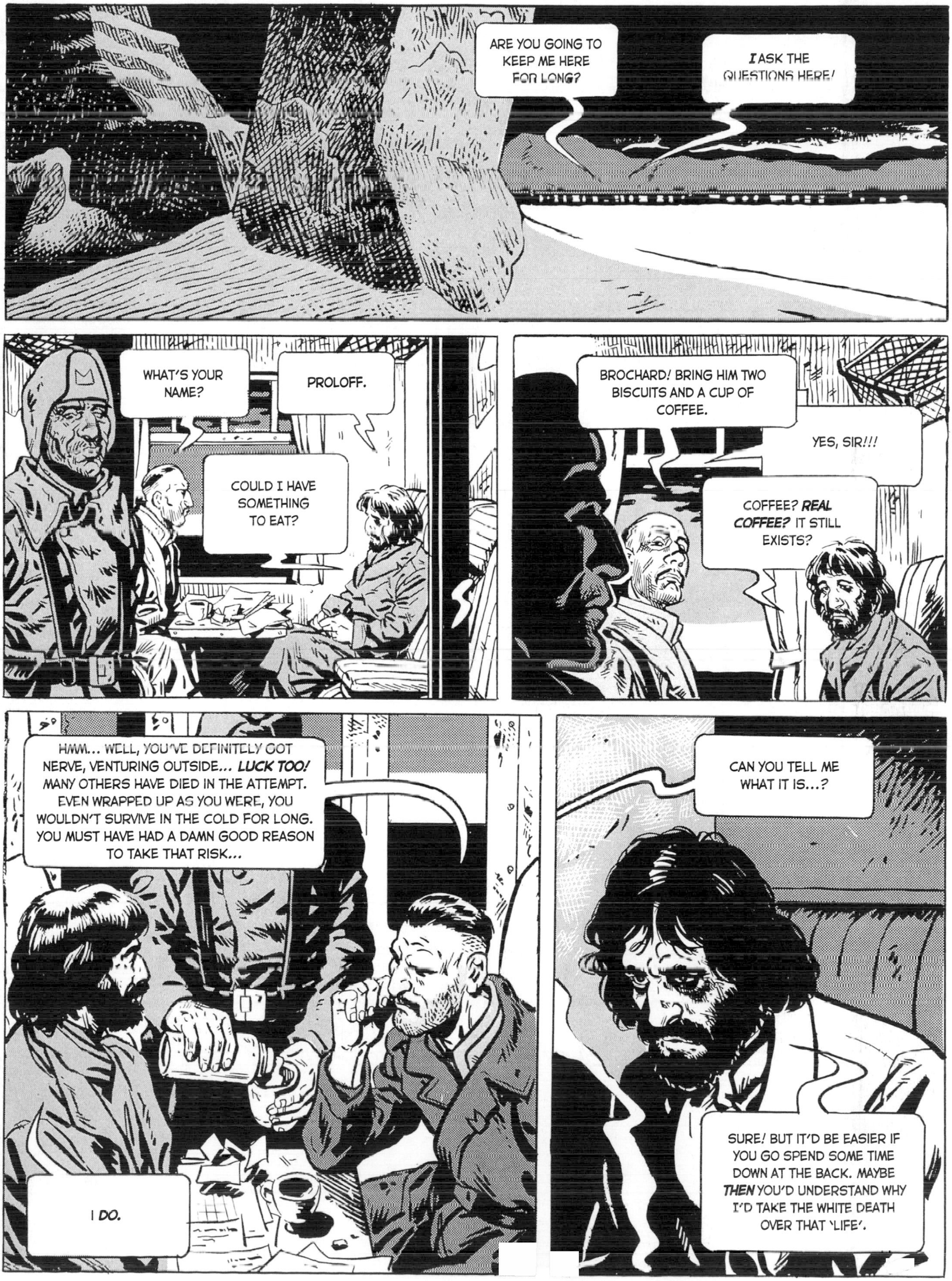
ARE YOU GOING TO KEEP ME HERE FOR LONG?
I ASK THE QUESTIONS HERE!
WHAT'S YOUR NAME?
PROLOFF.
COULD I HAVE SOMETHING TO EAT?
BROCHARD! BRING HIM TWO BISCUITS AND A CUP OF COFFEE.
YES, SIR!!!
COFFEE? REAL COFFEE? IT STILL EXISTS?
HMM... WELL, YOU'VE DEFINITELY GOT NERVE, VENTURING OUTSIDE... LUCK TOO! MANY OTHERS HAVE DIED IN THE ATTEMPT. EVEN WRAPPED UP AS YOU WERE, YOU WOULDN'T SURVIVE IN THE COLD FOR LONG. YOU MUST HAVE HAD A DAMN GOOD REASON TO TAKE THAT RISK...
I DO.
CAN YOU TELL ME WHAT IT IS...?
SURE! BUT IT'D BE EASIER IF YOU GO SPEND SOME TIME DOWN AT THE BACK. MAYBE THEN YOU'D UNDERSTAND WHY I'D TAKE THE WHITE DEATH OVER THAT 'LIFE'.

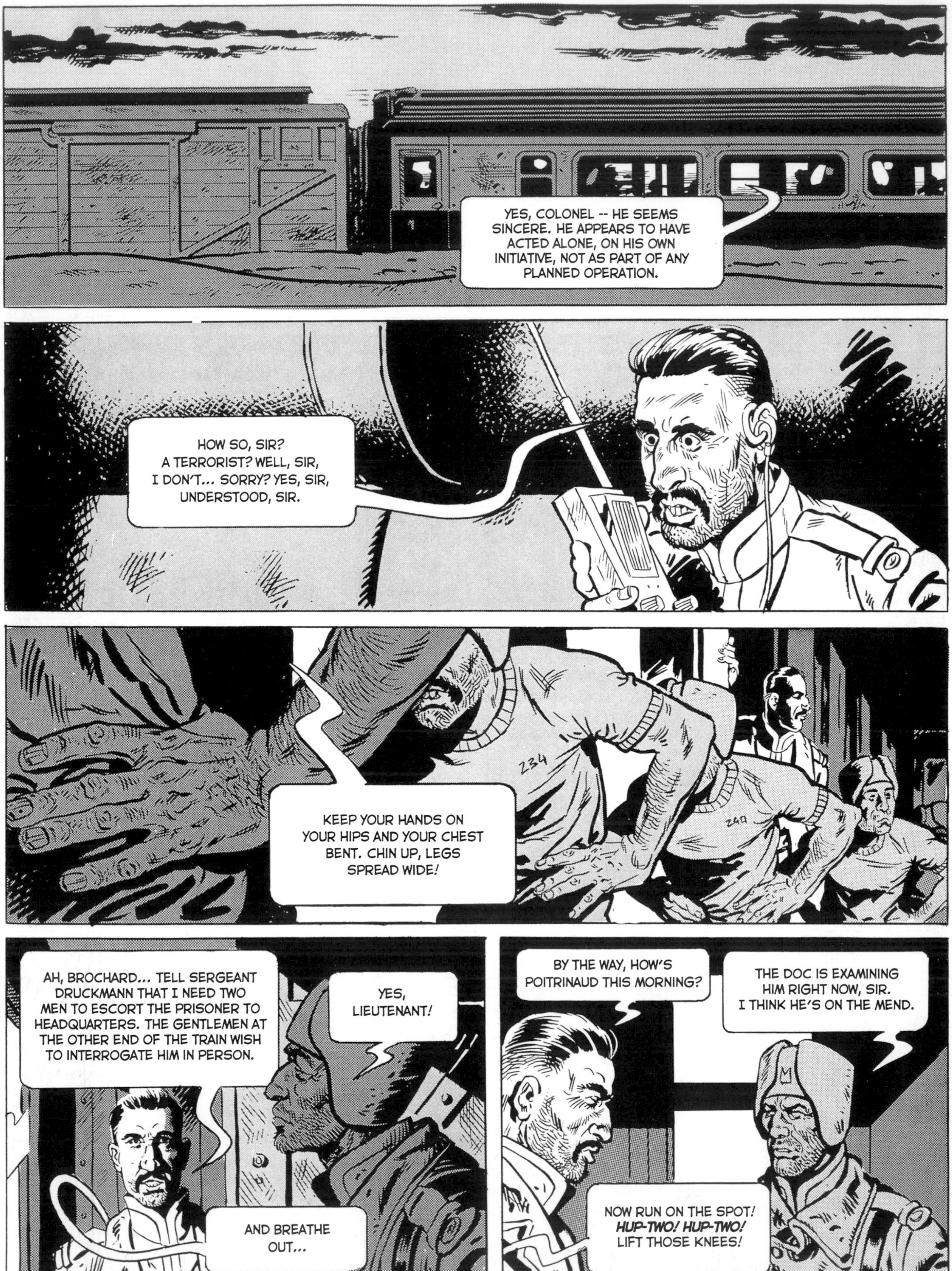
YES, COLONEL -- HE SEEMS SINCERE. HE APPEARS TO HAVE ACTED ALONE, ON HIS OWN INITIATIVE, NOT AS PART OF ANY PLANNED OPERATION.
HOW SO, SIR? A TERRORIST? WELL, SIR, I DON'T... SORRY? YES, SIR, UNDERSTOOD, SIR.
KEEP YOUR HANDS ON YOUR HIPS AND YOUR CHEST BENT. CHIN UP, LEGS SPREAD WIDE!
AH, BROCHARD... TELL SERGEANT DRUCKMANN THAT I NEED TWO MEN TO ESCORT THE PRISONER TO HEADQUARTERS. THE GENTLEMEN AT THE OTHER END OF THE TRAIN WISH TO INTERROGATE HIM IN PERSON.
YES, LIEUTENANT!
AND BREATHE OUT...
BY THE WAY, HOW'S POITRINAUD THIS MORNING?
THE DOC IS EXAMINING HIM RIGHT NOW, SIR. I THINK HE'S ON THE MEND.
NOW RUN ON THE SPOT! ***HUP-TWO! HUP-TWO!*** LIFT THOSE KNEES!

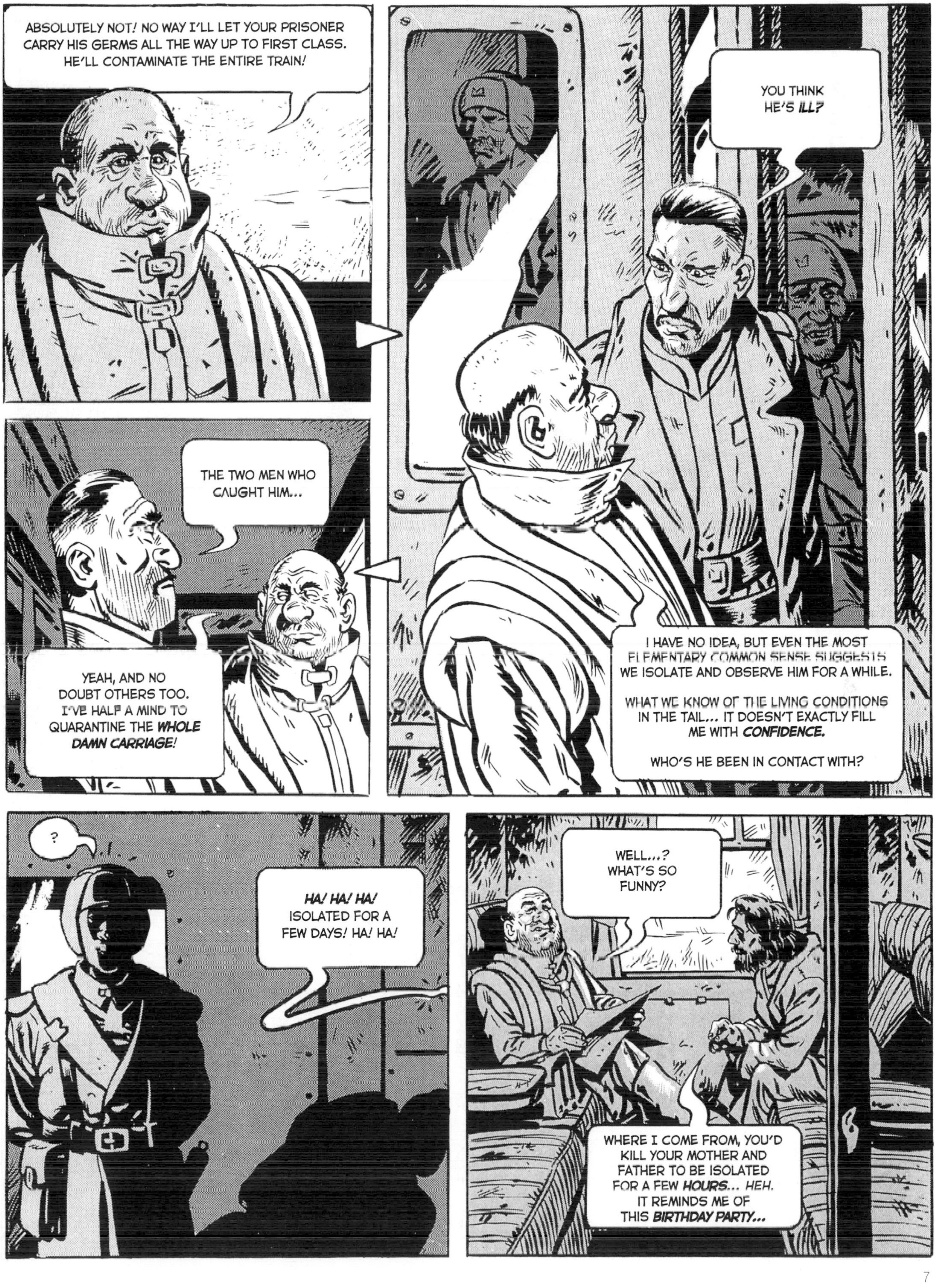
ABSOLUTELY NOT! NO WAY I'LL LET YOUR PRISONER CARRY HIS GERMS ALL THE WAY UP TO FIRST CLASS. HE'LL CONTAMINATE THE ENTIRE TRAIN!
YOU THINK HE'S ILL?
I HAVE NO IDEA, BUT EVEN THE MOST ELEMENTARY COMMON SENSE SUGGESTS WE ISOLATE AND OBSERVE HIM FOR A WHILE.
WHAT WE KNOW OF THE LIVING CONDITIONS IN THE TAIL... IT DOESN'T EXACTLY FILL ME WITH CONFIDENCE.
WHO'S HE BEEN IN CONTACT WITH?
THE TWO MEN WHO CAUGHT HIM...
YEAH, AND NO DOUBT OTHERS TOO. I'VE HALF A MIND TO QUARANTINE THE WHOLE DAMN CARRIAGE!
?
HA! HA! HA! ISOLATED FOR A FEW DAYS! HA! HA!
WELL...? WHAT'S SO FUNNY?
WHERE I COME FROM, YOU'D KILL YOUR MOTHER AND FATHER TO BE ISOLATED FOR A FEW HOURS... HEH. IT REMINDS ME OF THIS BIRTHDAY PARTY...

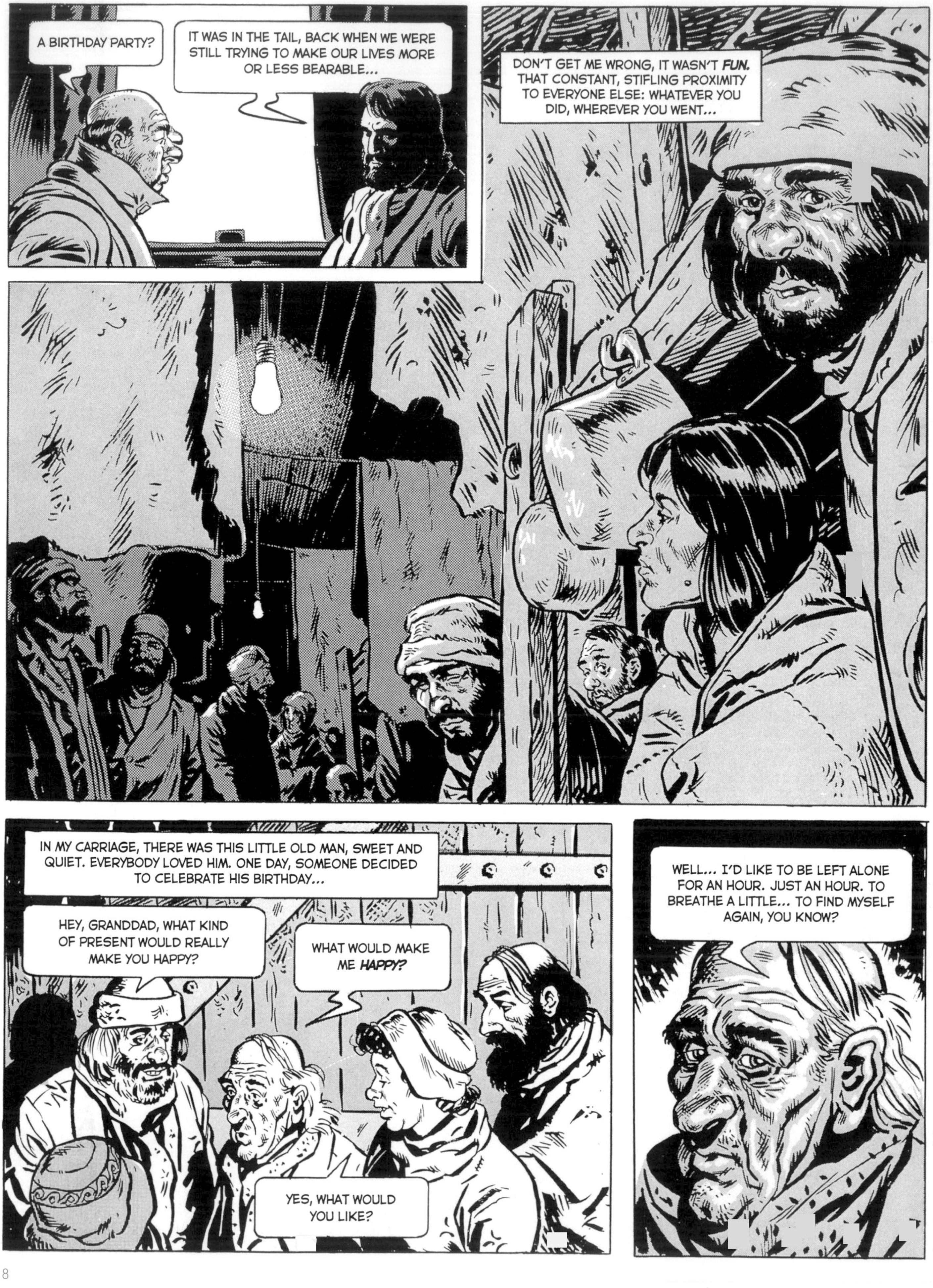
A BIRTHDAY PARTY?
IT WAS IN THE TAIL, BACK WHEN WE WERE STILL TRYING TO MAKE OUR LIVES MORE OR LESS BEARABLE...
DON'T GET ME WRONG, IT WASN'T *FUN.* THAT CONSTANT, STIFLING PROXIMITY TO EVERYONE ELSE: WHATEVER YOU DID, WHEREVER YOU WENT...
IN MY CARRIAGE, THERE WAS THIS LITTLE OLD MAN, SWEET AND QUIET. EVERYBODY LOVED HIM. ONE DAY, SOMEONE DECIDED TO CELEBRATE HIS BIRTHDAY...
HEY, GRANDDAD, WHAT KIND OF PRESENT WOULD REALLY MAKE YOU HAPPY?
WHAT WOULD MAKE ME *HAPPY?*
YES, WHAT WOULD YOU LIKE?
WELL... I'D LIKE TO BE LEFT ALONE FOR AN HOUR. JUST AN HOUR. TO BREATHE A LITTLE... TO FIND MYSELF AGAIN, YOU KNOW?

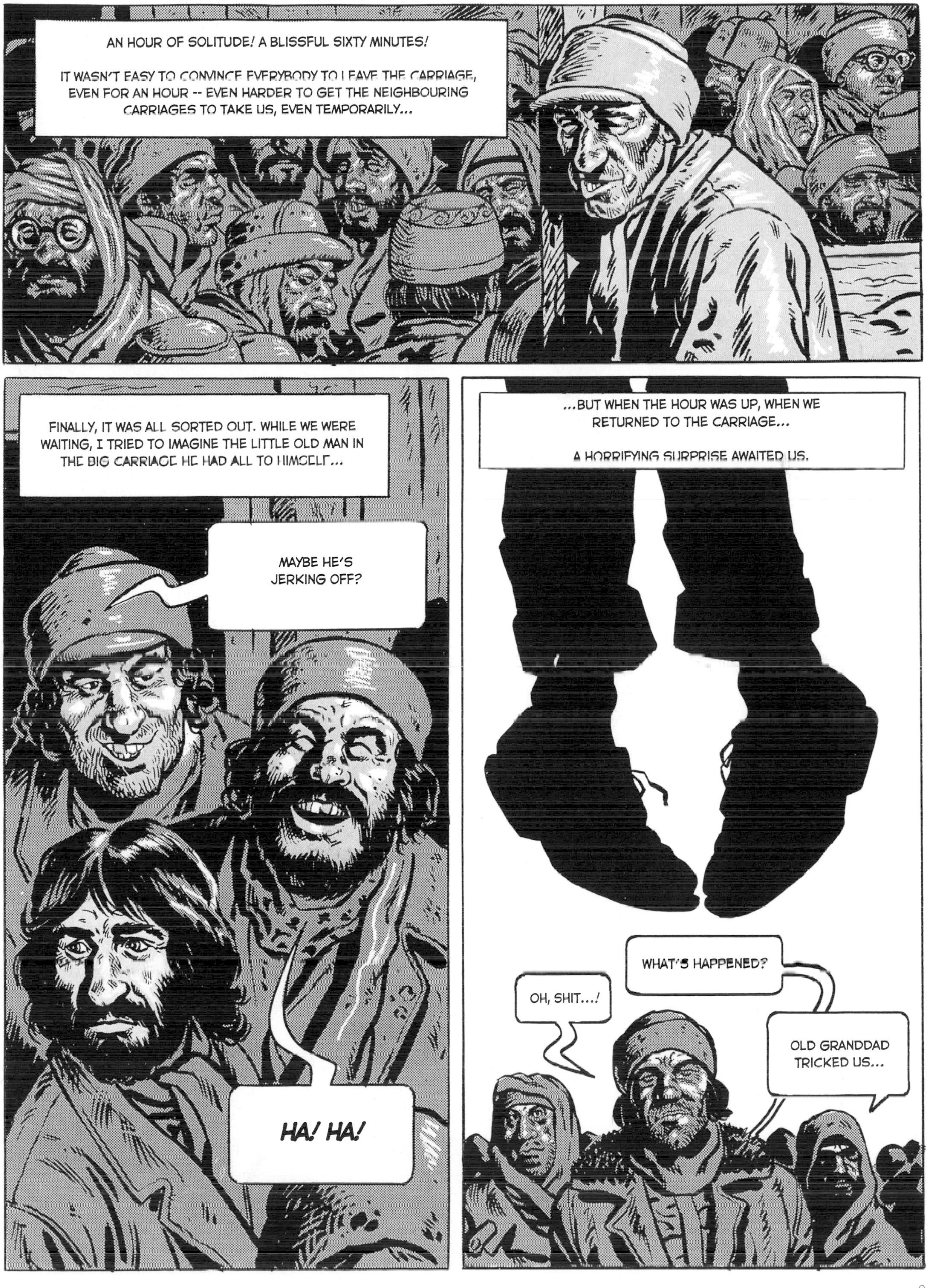
AN HOUR OF SOLITUDE! A BLISSFUL SIXTY MINUTES!
IT WASN'T EASY TO CONVINCE EVERYBODY TO LEAVE THE CARRIAGE, EVEN FOR AN HOUR -- EVEN HARDER TO GET THE NEIGHBOURING CARRIAGES TO TAKE US, EVEN TEMPORARILY...
FINALLY, IT WAS ALL SORTED OUT. WHILE WE WERE WAITING, I TRIED TO IMAGINE THE LITTLE OLD MAN IN THE BIG CARRIAGE HE HAD ALL TO HIMSELF...
MAYBE HE'S JERKING OFF?
HA! HA!
...BUT WHEN THE HOUR WAS UP, WHEN WE RETURNED TO THE CARRIAGE...
A HORRIFYING SURPRISE AWAITED US.
OH, SHIT...!
WHAT'S HAPPENED?
OLD GRANDDAD TRICKED US...

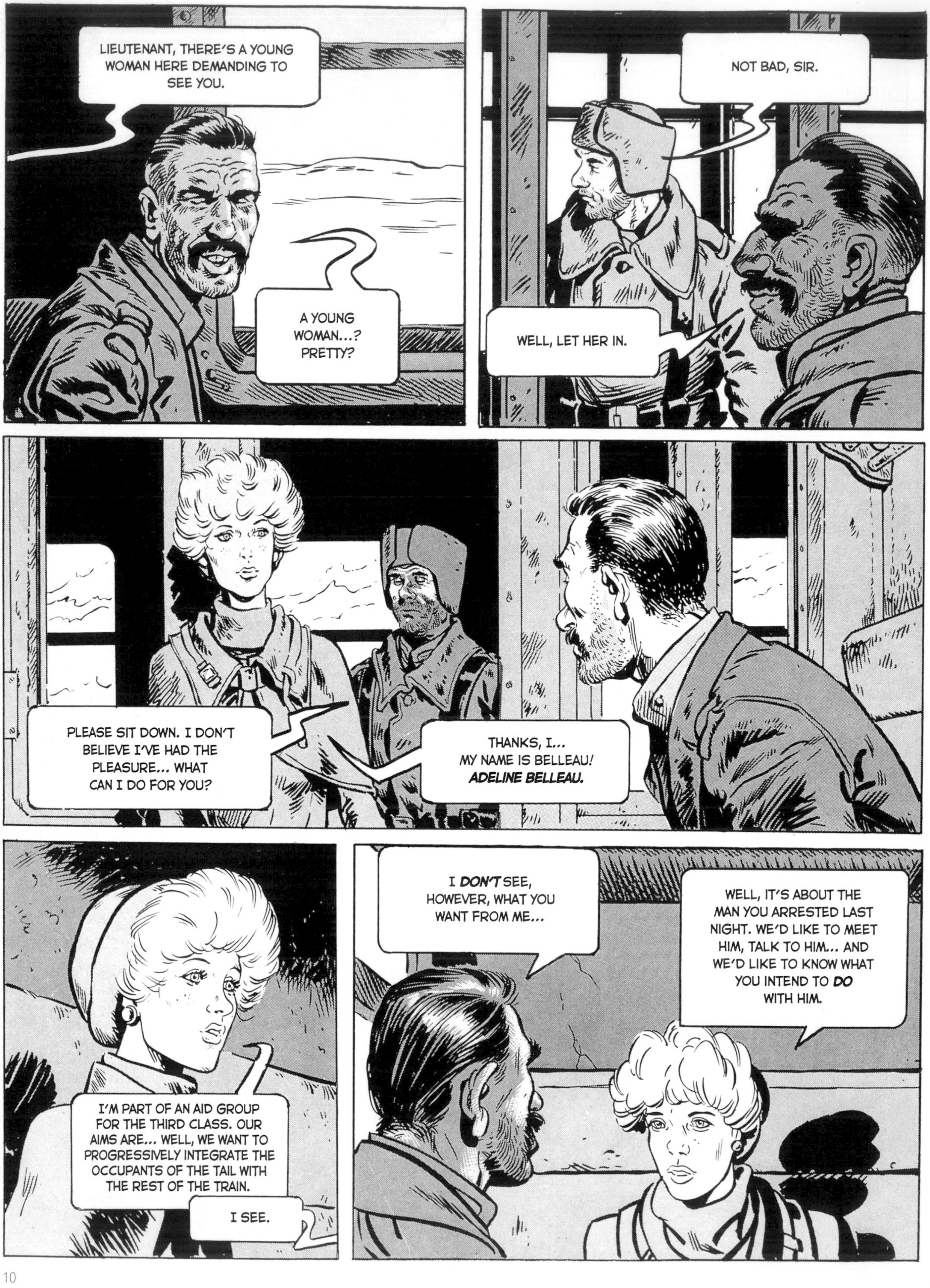
LIEUTENANT, THERE'S A YOUNG WOMAN HERE DEMANDING TO SEE YOU.
A YOUNG WOMAN...? PRETTY?
NOT BAD, SIR.
WELL, LET HER IN.
PLEASE SIT DOWN. I DON'T BELIEVE I'VE HAD THE PLEASURE... WHAT CAN I DO FOR YOU?
THANKS, I... MY NAME IS BELLEAU! ***ADELINE BELLEAU.***
I'M PART OF AN AID GROUP FOR THE THIRD CLASS. OUR AIMS ARE... WELL, WE WANT TO PROGRESSIVELY INTEGRATE THE OCCUPANTS OF THE TAIL WITH THE REST OF THE TRAIN.
I SEE.
I ***DON'T*** SEE, HOWEVER, WHAT YOU WANT FROM ME...
WELL, IT'S ABOUT THE MAN YOU ARRESTED LAST NIGHT. WE'D LIKE TO MEET HIM, TALK TO HIM... AND WE'D LIKE TO KNOW WHAT YOU INTEND TO ***DO*** WITH HIM.

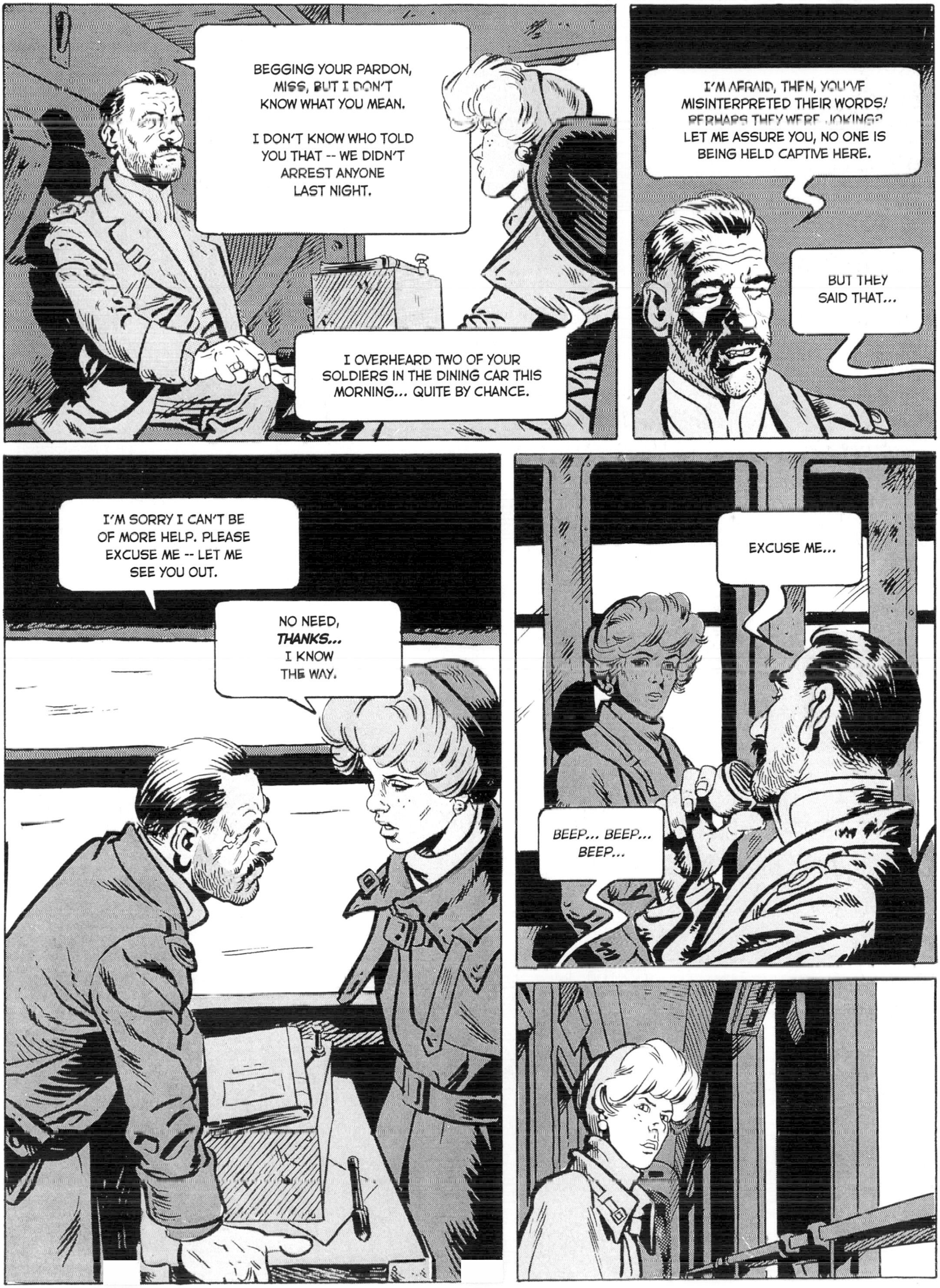
BEGGING YOUR PARDON, MISS, BUT I DON'T KNOW WHAT YOU MEAN.
I DON'T KNOW WHO TOLD YOU THAT -- WE DIDN'T ARREST ANYONE LAST NIGHT.
I OVERHEARD TWO OF YOUR SOLDIERS IN THE DINING CAR THIS MORNING... QUITE BY CHANCE.
I'M AFRAID, THEN, YOU'VE MISINTERPRETED THEIR WORDS! PERHAPS THEY WERE JOKING? LET ME ASSURE YOU, NO ONE IS BEING HELD CAPTIVE HERE.
BUT THEY SAID THAT...
I'M SORRY I CAN'T BE OF MORE HELP. PLEASE EXCUSE ME -- LET ME SEE YOU OUT.
NO NEED, *THANKS...* I KNOW THE WAY.
EXCUSE ME...
BEEP... BEEP... BEEP...

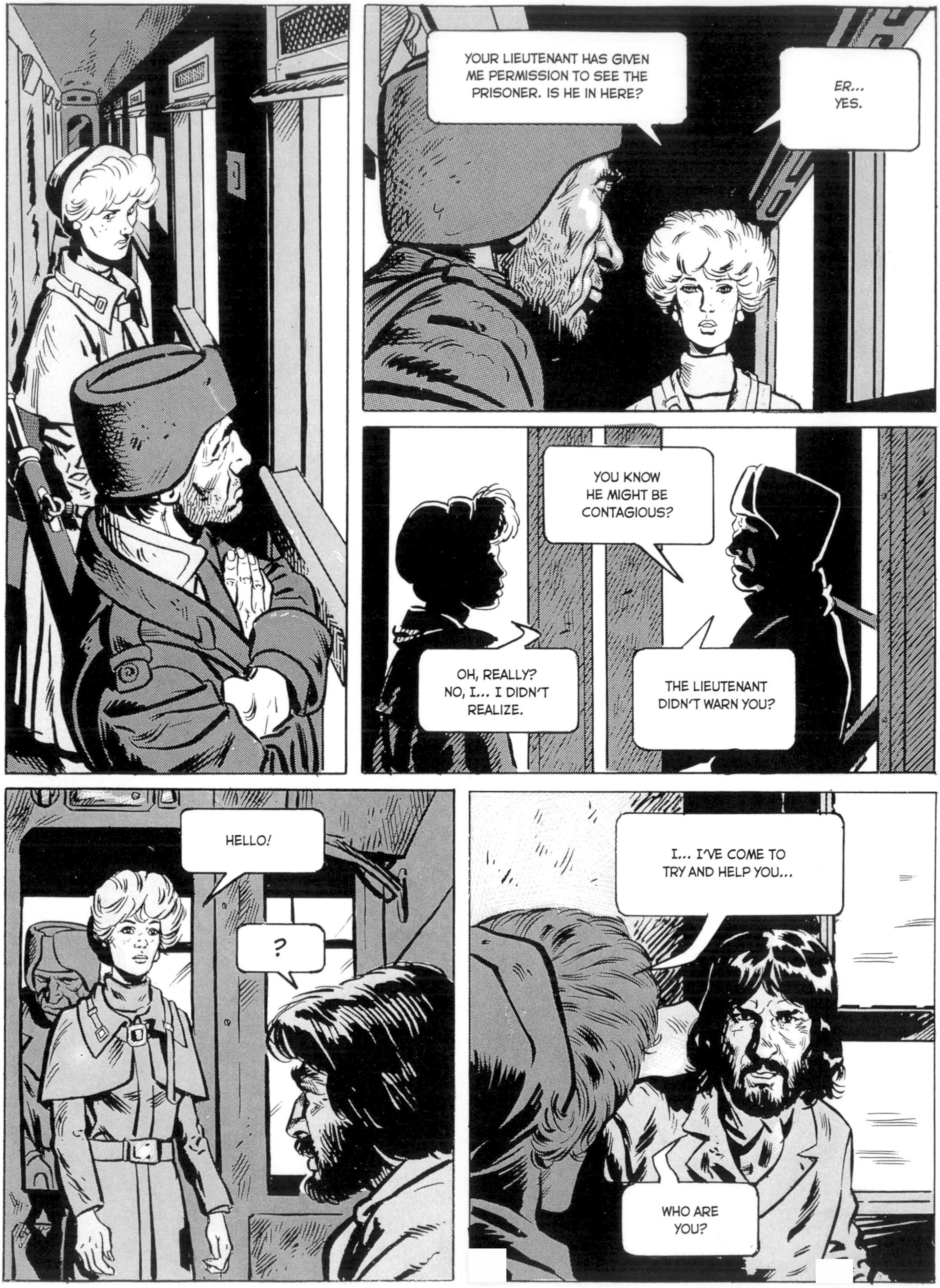
YOUR LIEUTENANT HAS GIVEN ME PERMISSION TO SEE THE PRISONER. IS HE IN HERE?
ER... YES.
YOU KNOW HE MIGHT BE CONTAGIOUS?
OH, REALLY? NO, I... I DIDN'T REALIZE.
THE LIEUTENANT DIDN'T WARN YOU?
HELLO!
?
I... I'VE COME TO TRY AND HELP YOU...
WHO ARE YOU?

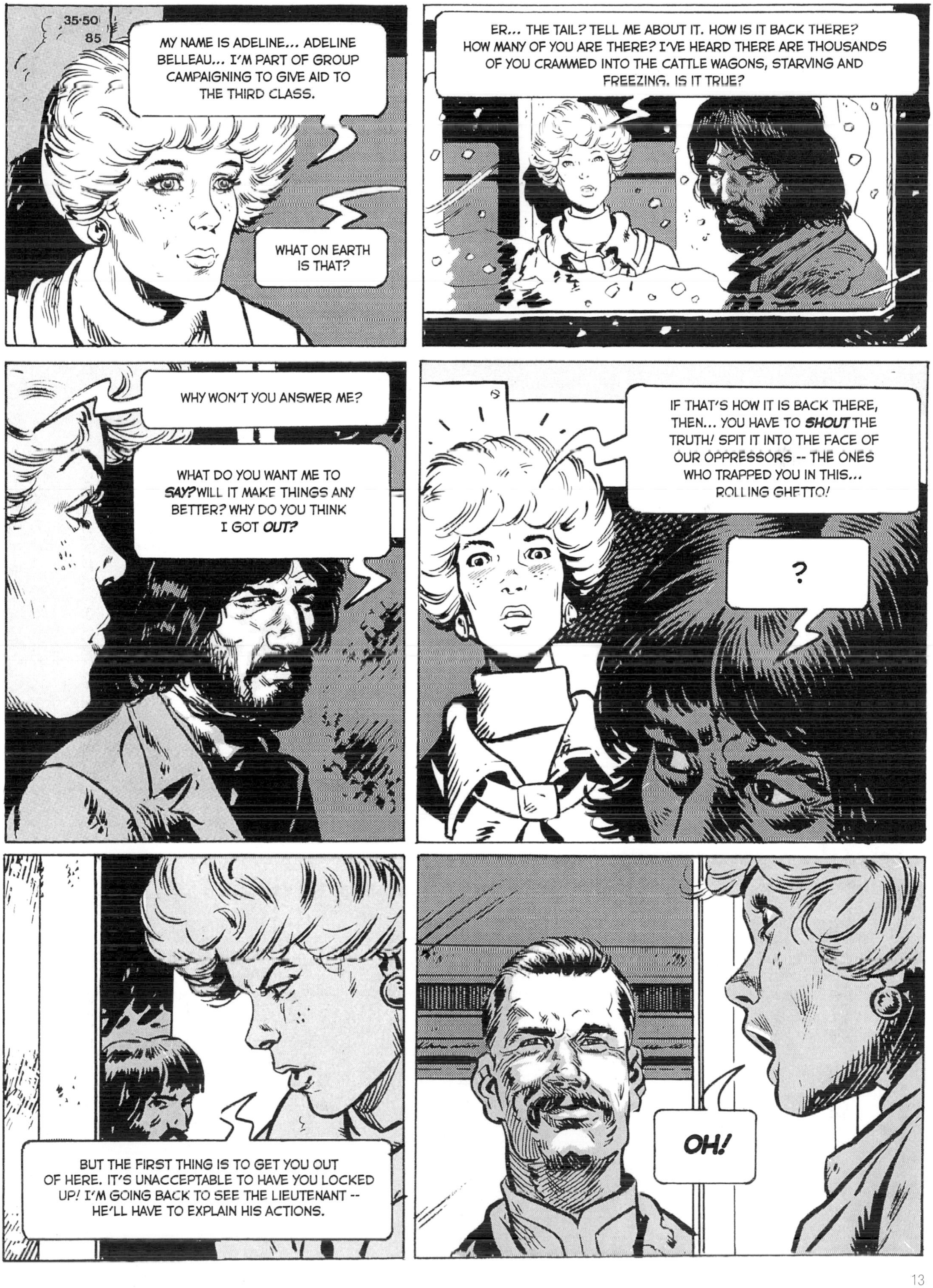
35·50
85
MY NAME IS ADELINE... ADELINE BELLEAU... I'M PART OF GROUP CAMPAIGNING TO GIVE AID TO THE THIRD CLASS.
WHAT ON EARTH IS THAT?
ER... THE TAIL? TELL ME ABOUT IT. HOW IS IT BACK THERE? HOW MANY OF YOU ARE THERE? I'VE HEARD THERE ARE THOUSANDS OF YOU CRAMMED INTO THE CATTLE WAGONS, STARVING AND FREEZING. IS IT TRUE?
WHY WON'T YOU ANSWER ME?
WHAT DO YOU WANT ME TO SAY? WILL IT MAKE THINGS ANY BETTER? WHY DO YOU THINK I GOT OUT?
IF THAT'S HOW IT IS BACK THERE, THEN... YOU HAVE TO SHOUT THE TRUTH! SPIT IT INTO THE FACE OF OUR OPPRESSORS -- THE ONES WHO TRAPPED YOU IN THIS... ROLLING GHETTO!
?
BUT THE FIRST THING IS TO GET YOU OUT OF HERE. IT'S UNACCEPTABLE TO HAVE YOU LOCKED UP! I'M GOING BACK TO SEE THE LIEUTENANT -- HE'LL HAVE TO EXPLAIN HIS ACTIONS.
OH!

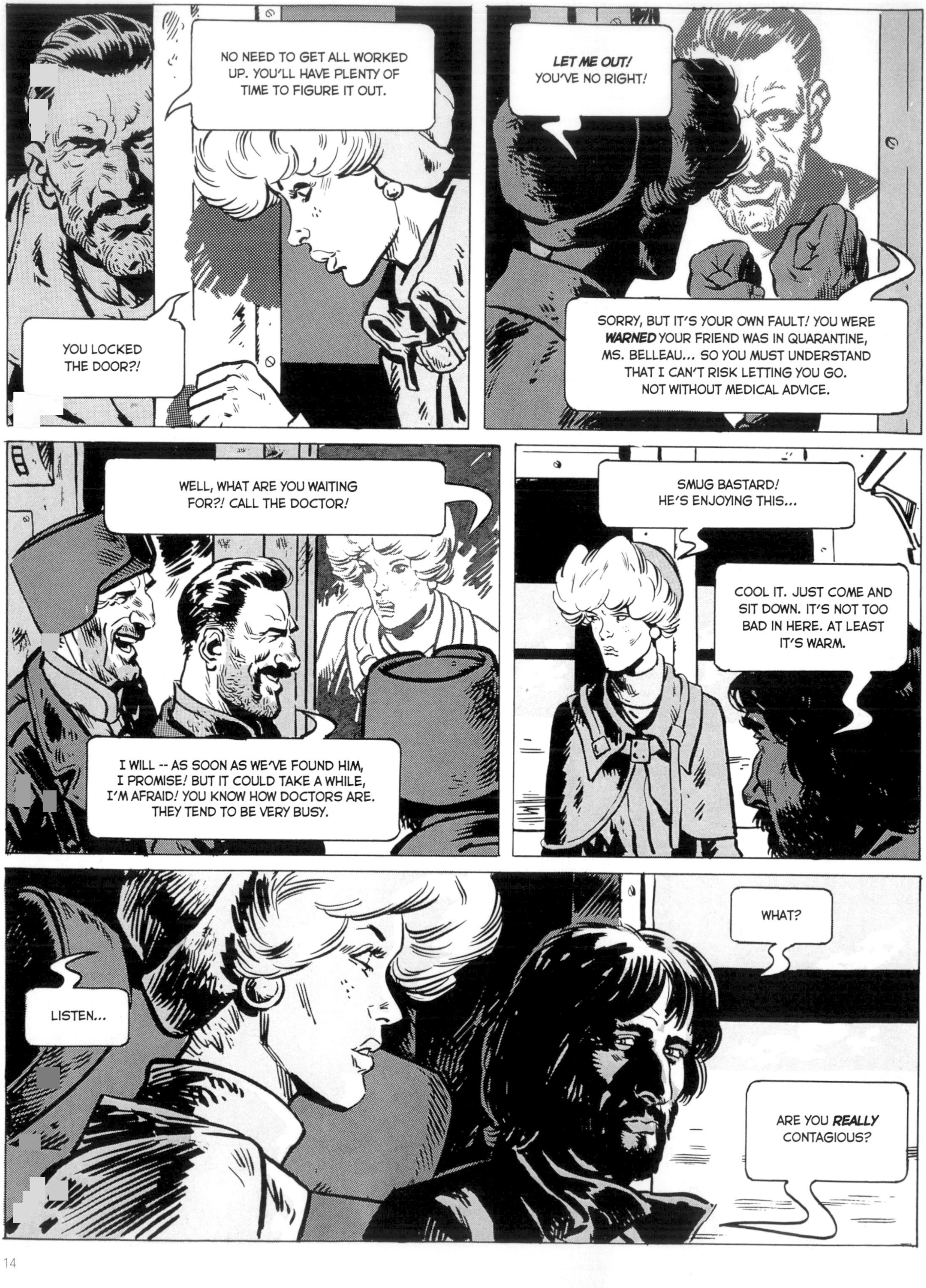

NO NEED TO GET ALL WORKED UP. YOU'LL HAVE PLENTY OF TIME TO FIGURE IT OUT.
YOU LOCKED THE DOOR?!
LET ME OUT! YOU'VE NO RIGHT!
SORRY, BUT IT'S YOUR OWN FAULT! YOU WERE WARNED YOUR FRIEND WAS IN QUARANTINE, MS. BELLEAU... SO YOU MUST UNDERSTAND THAT I CAN'T RISK LETTING YOU GO. NOT WITHOUT MEDICAL ADVICE.
WELL, WHAT ARE YOU WAITING FOR?! CALL THE DOCTOR!
I WILL -- AS SOON AS WE'VE FOUND HIM, I PROMISE! BUT IT COULD TAKE A WHILE, I'M AFRAID! YOU KNOW HOW DOCTORS ARE. THEY TEND TO BE VERY BUSY.
SMUG BASTARD! HE'S ENJOYING THIS...
COOL IT. JUST COME AND SIT DOWN. IT'S NOT TOO BAD IN HERE. AT LEAST IT'S WARM.
LISTEN...
WHAT?
ARE YOU REALLY CONTAGIOUS?

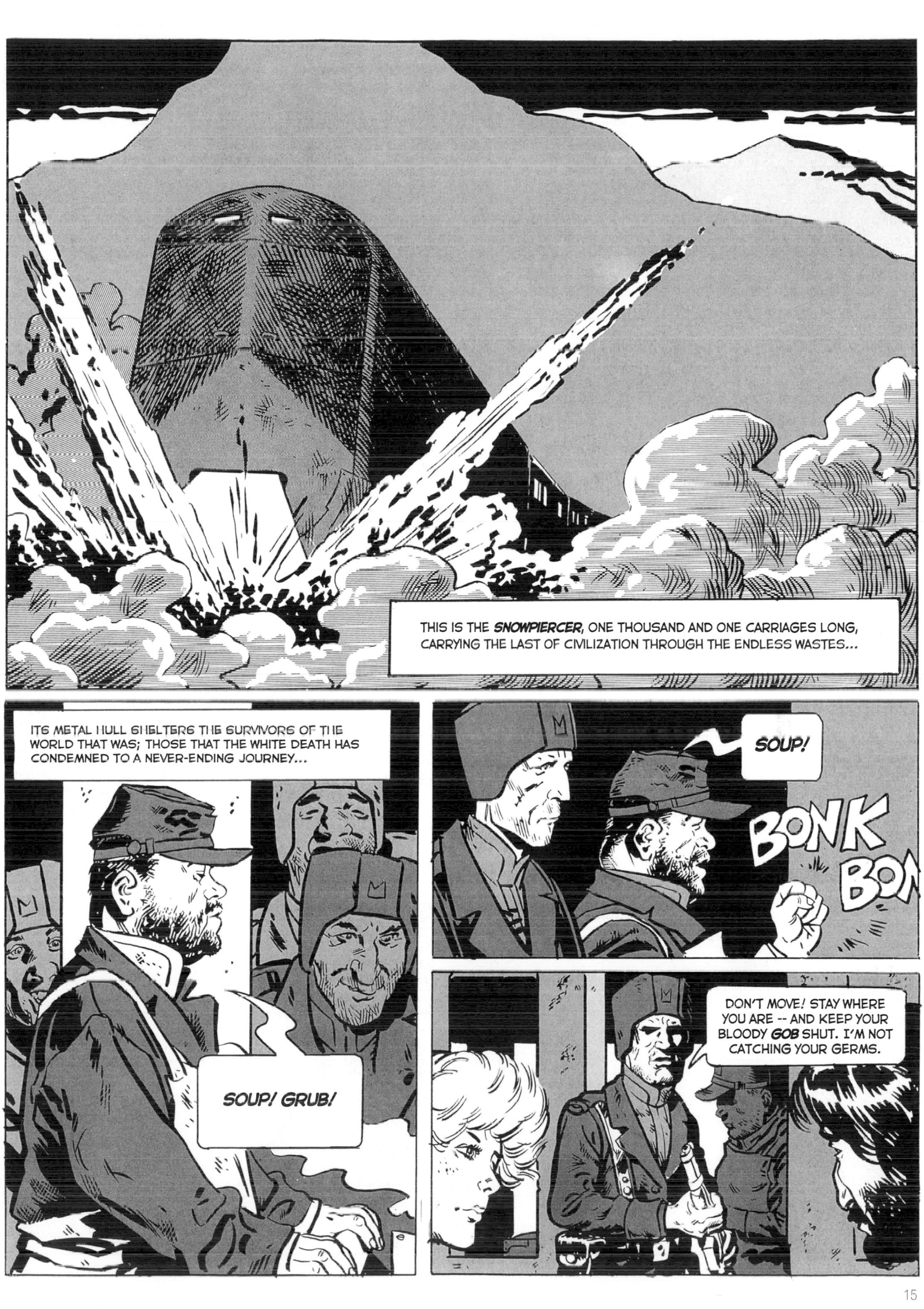
THIS IS THE SNOWPIERCER, ONE THOUSAND AND ONE CARRIAGES LONG, CARRYING THE LAST OF CIVILIZATION THROUGH THE ENDLESS WASTES...
ITS METAL HULL SHELTERS THE SURVIVORS OF THE WORLD THAT WAS; THOSE THAT THE WHITE DEATH HAS CONDEMNED TO A NEVER-ENDING JOURNEY...
SOUP! GRUB!
SOUP!
BONK
DON'T MOVE! STAY WHERE YOU ARE -- AND KEEP YOUR BLOODY GOB SHUT. I'M NOT CATCHING YOUR GERMS.

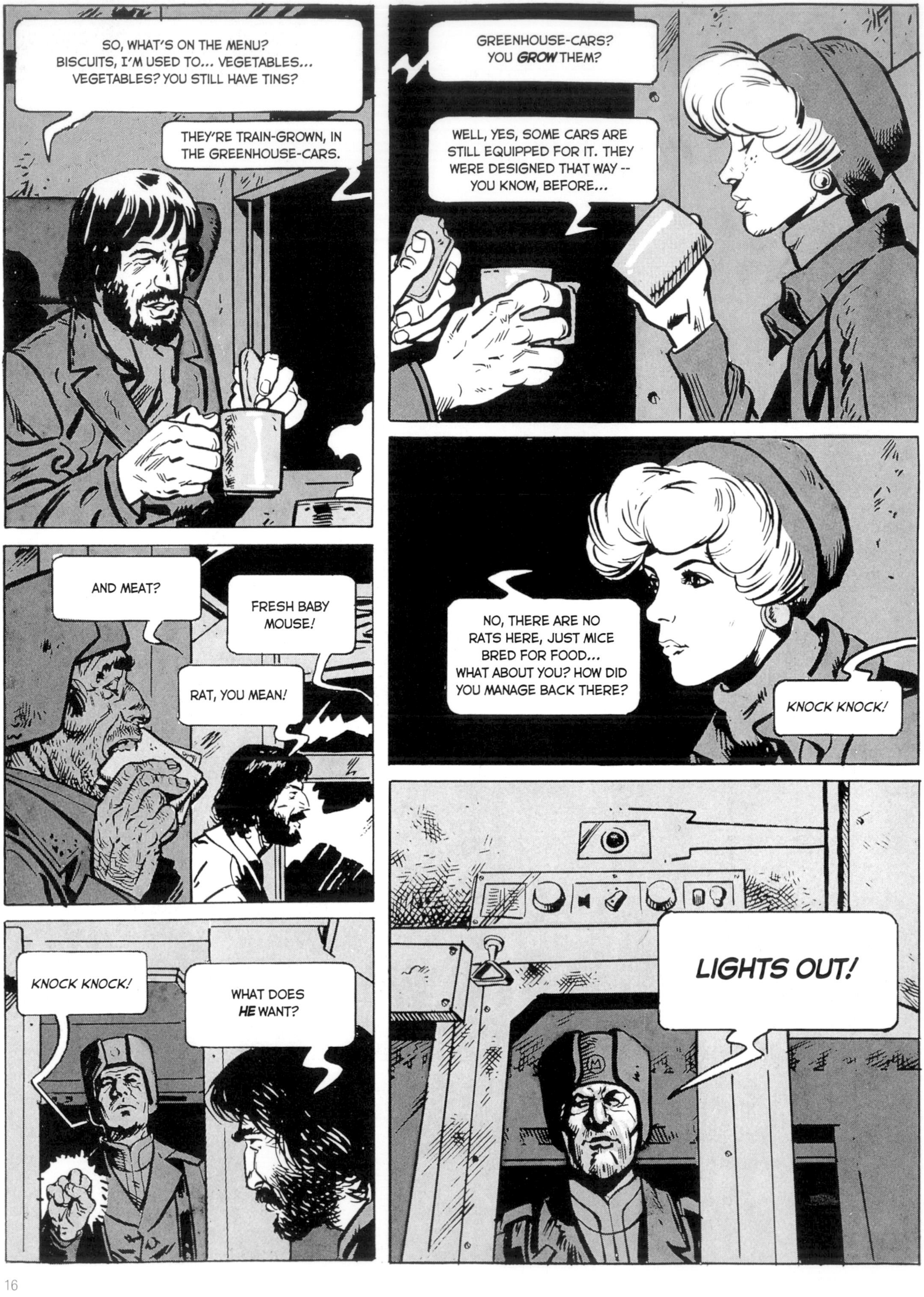
SO, WHAT'S ON THE MENU? BISCUITS, I'M USED TO... VEGETABLES... VEGETABLES? YOU STILL HAVE TINS?
THEY'RE TRAIN-GROWN, IN THE GREENHOUSE-CARS.
GREENHOUSE-CARS? YOU GROW THEM?
WELL, YES, SOME CARS ARE STILL EQUIPPED FOR IT. THEY WERE DESIGNED THAT WAY -- YOU KNOW, BEFORE...
AND MEAT?
FRESH BABY MOUSE!
RAT, YOU MEAN!
NO, THERE ARE NO RATS HERE, JUST MICE BRED FOR FOOD... WHAT ABOUT YOU? HOW DID YOU MANAGE BACK THERE?
KNOCK KNOCK!
KNOCK KNOCK!
WHAT DOES HE WANT?
LIGHTS OUT!

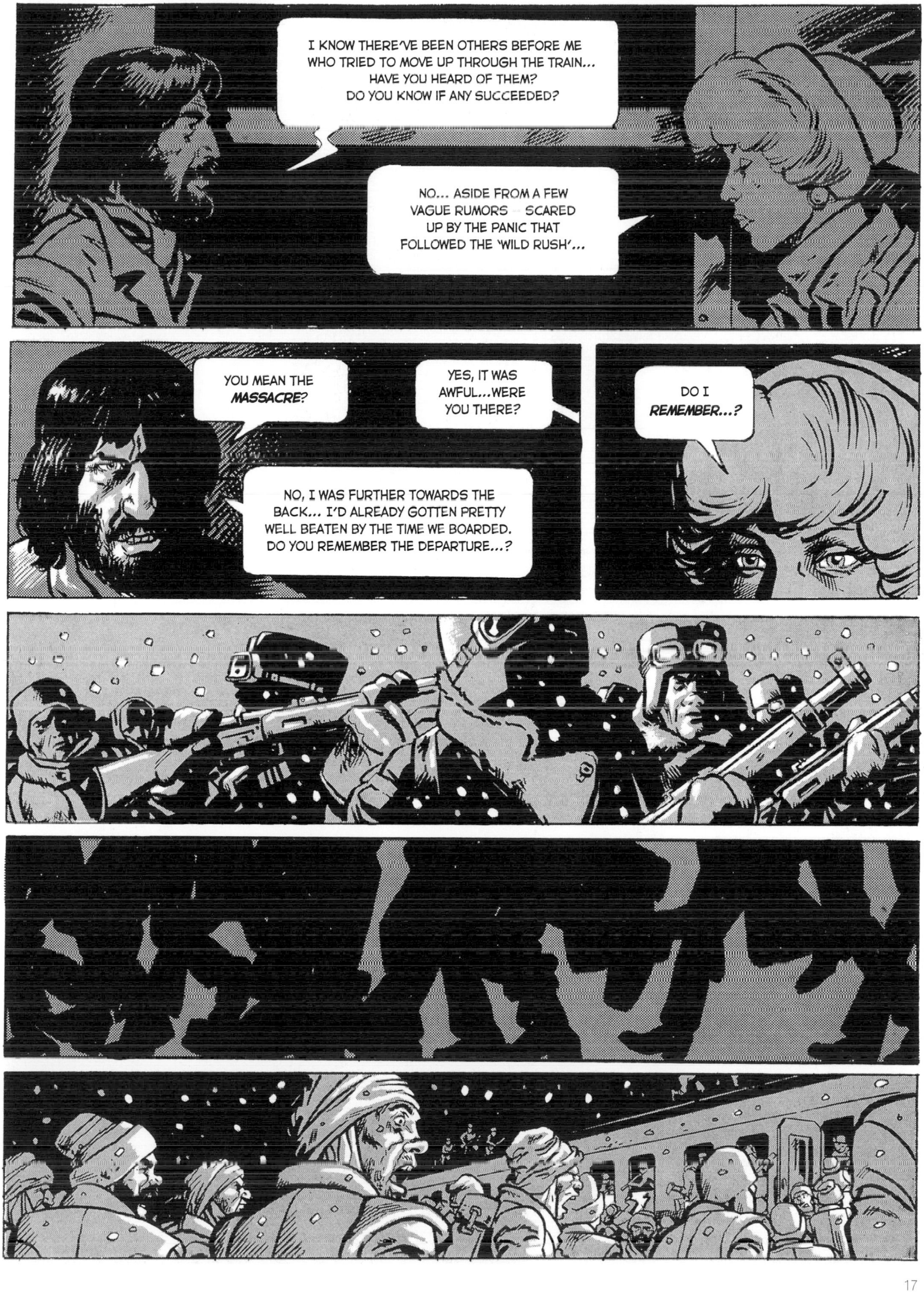

I KNOW THERE'VE BEEN OTHERS BEFORE ME WHO TRIED TO MOVE UP THROUGH THE TRAIN... HAVE YOU HEARD OF THEM? DO YOU KNOW IF ANY SUCCEEDED?
NO... ASIDE FROM A FEW VAGUE RUMORS — SCARED UP BY THE PANIC THAT FOLLOWED THE 'WILD RUSH'...
YOU MEAN THE MASSACRE?
YES, IT WAS AWFUL...WERE YOU THERE?
NO, I WAS FURTHER TOWARDS THE BACK... I'D ALREADY GOTTEN PRETTY WELL BEATEN BY THE TIME WE BOARDED. DO YOU REMEMBER THE DEPARTURE...?
DO I REMEMBER...?

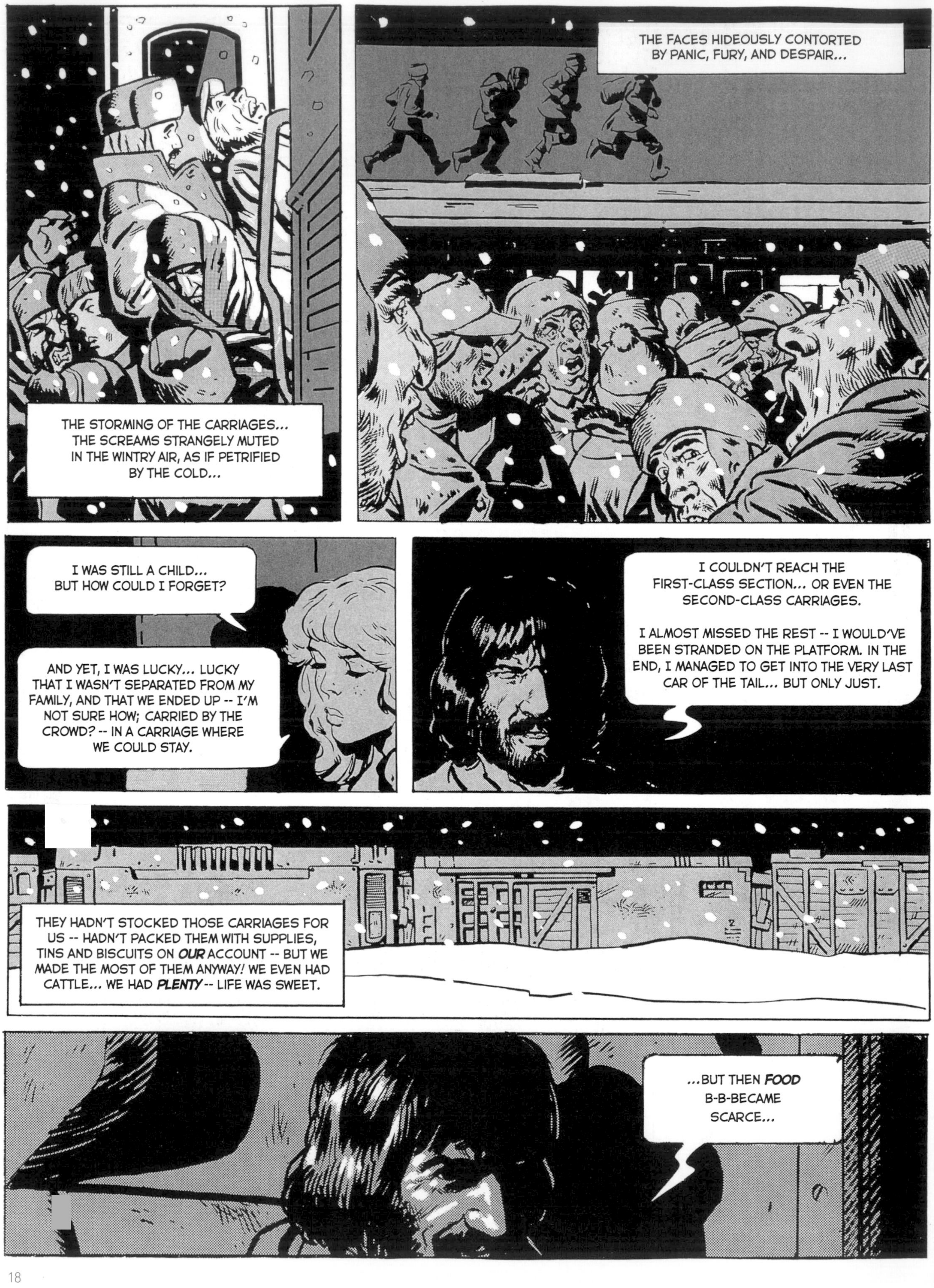
THE STORMING OF THE CARRIAGES... THE SCREAMS STRANGELY MUTED IN THE WINTRY AIR, AS IF PETRIFIED BY THE COLD...
THE FACES HIDEOUSLY CONTORTED BY PANIC, FURY, AND DESPAIR...
I WAS STILL A CHILD... BUT HOW COULD I FORGET?
AND YET, I WAS LUCKY... LUCKY THAT I WASN'T SEPARATED FROM MY FAMILY, AND THAT WE ENDED UP -- I'M NOT SURE HOW; CARRIED BY THE CROWD? -- IN A CARRIAGE WHERE WE COULD STAY.
I COULDN'T REACH THE FIRST-CLASS SECTION... OR EVEN THE SECOND-CLASS CARRIAGES.
I ALMOST MISSED THE REST -- I WOULD'VE BEEN STRANDED ON THE PLATFORM. IN THE END, I MANAGED TO GET INTO THE VERY LAST CAR OF THE TAIL... BUT ONLY JUST.
THEY HADN'T STOCKED THOSE CARRIAGES FOR US -- HADN'T PACKED THEM WITH SUPPLIES, TINS AND BISCUITS ON *OUR* ACCOUNT -- BUT WE MADE THE MOST OF THEM ANYWAY! WE EVEN HAD CATTLE... WE HAD *PLENTY* -- LIFE WAS SWEET.
...BUT THEN *FOOD* B-B-BECAME SCARCE...

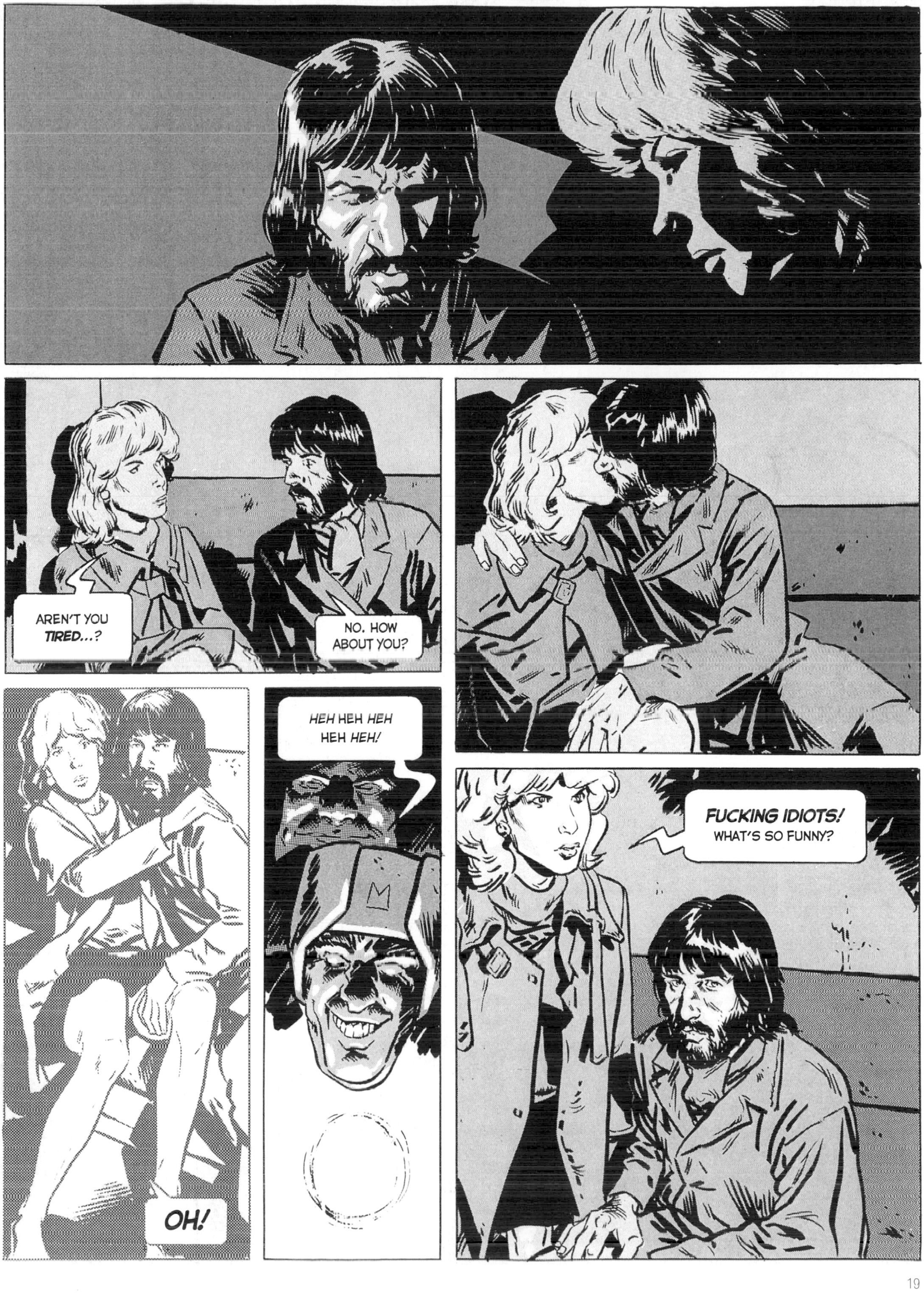

AREN'T YOU TIRED...?
NO. HOW ABOUT YOU?
OH!
HEH HEH HEH HEH HEH!
FUCKING IDIOTS! WHAT'S SO FUNNY?

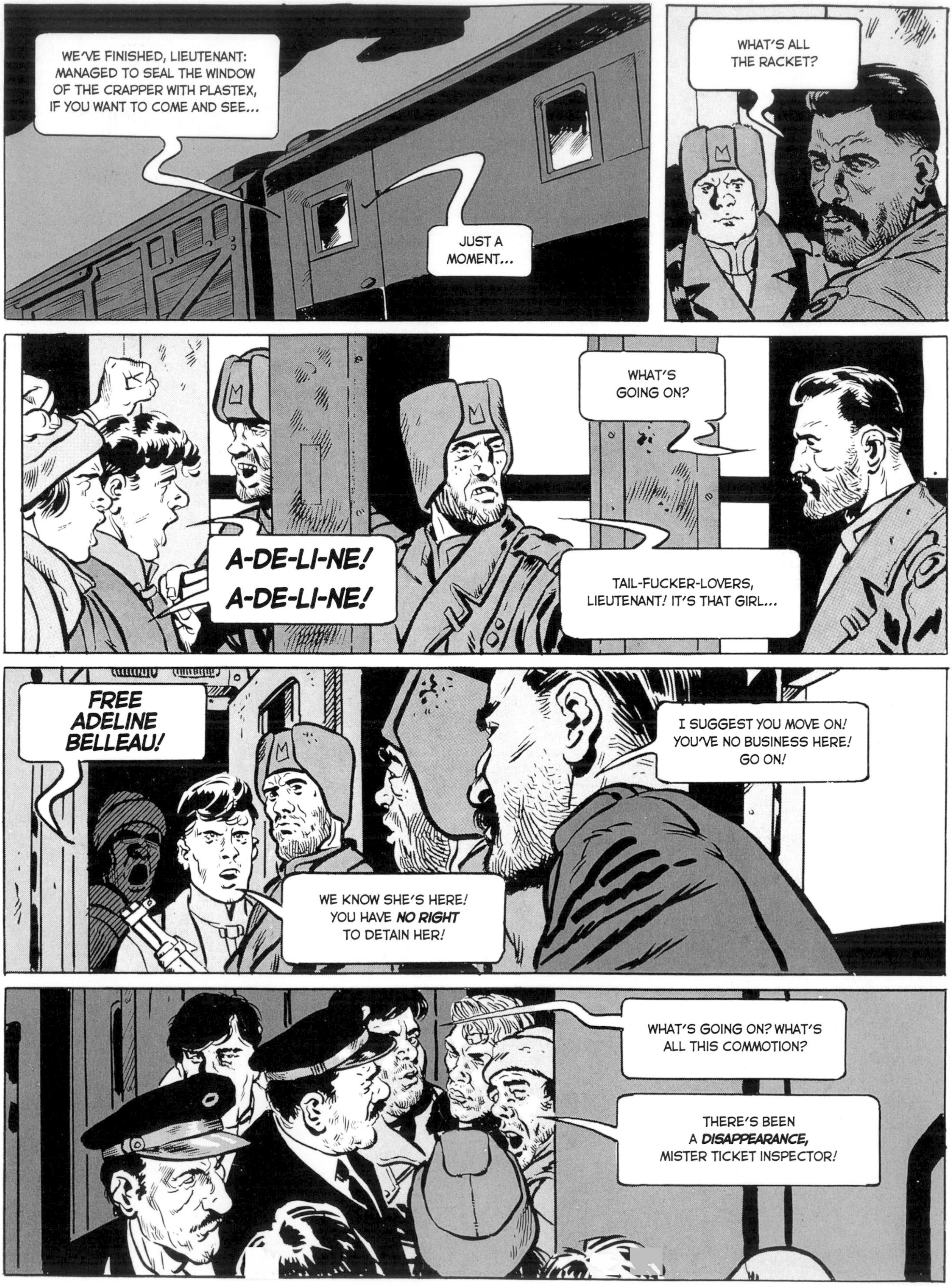
WE'VE FINISHED, LIEUTENANT: MANAGED TO SEAL THE WINDOW OF THE CRAPPER WITH PLASTEX, IF YOU WANT TO COME AND SEE...
JUST A MOMENT...
WHAT'S ALL THE RACKET?
A-DE-LI-NE! A-DE-LI-NE!
WHAT'S GOING ON?
TAIL-FUCKER-LOVERS, LIEUTENANT! IT'S THAT GIRL...
FREE ADELINE BELLEAU!
WE KNOW SHE'S HERE! YOU HAVE NO RIGHT TO DETAIN HER!
I SUGGEST YOU MOVE ON! YOU'VE NO BUSINESS HERE! GO ON!
WHAT'S GOING ON? WHAT'S ALL THIS COMMOTION?
THERE'S BEEN A DISAPPEARANCE, MISTER TICKET INSPECTOR!

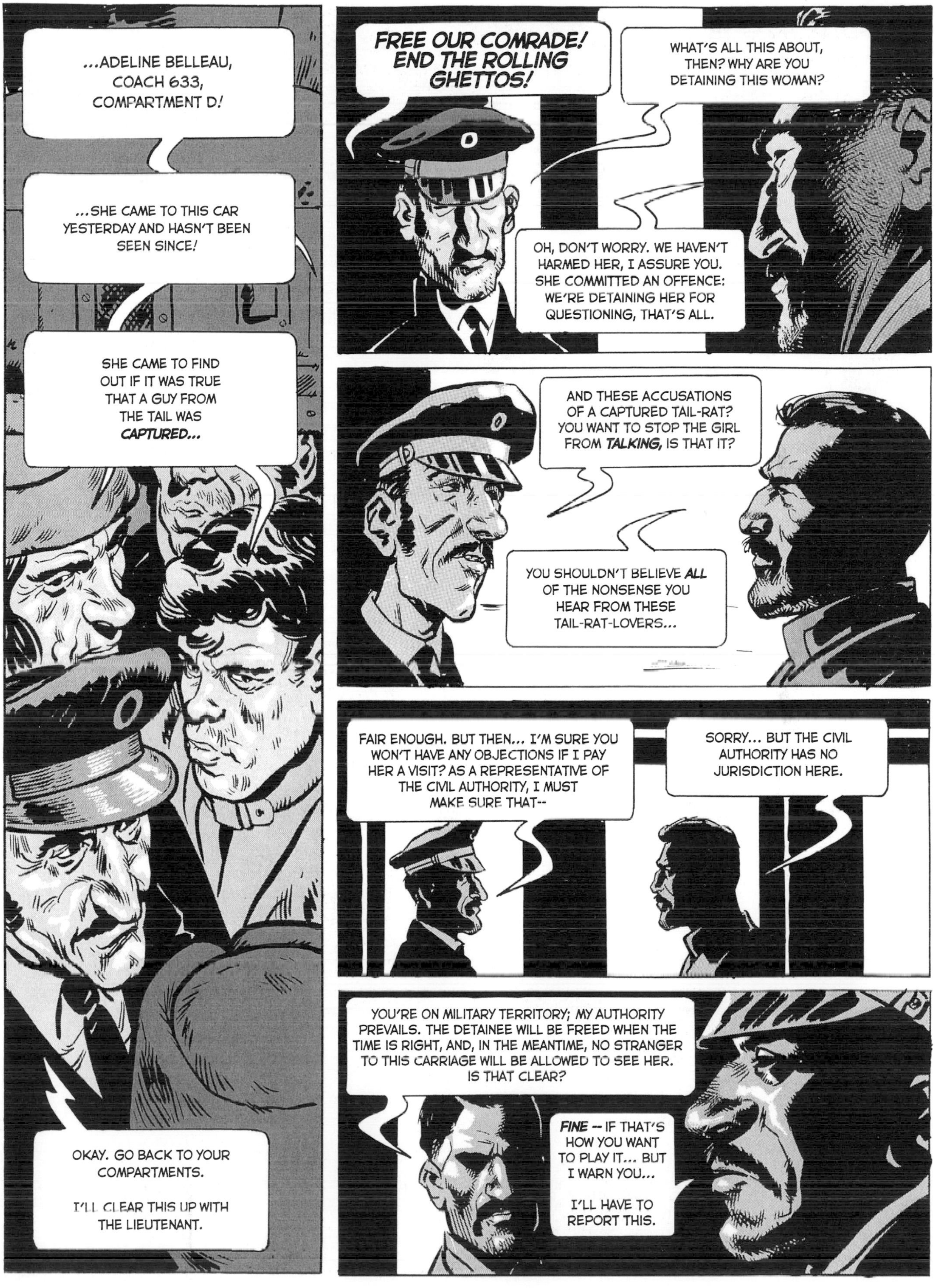
...ADELINE BELLEAU, COACH 633, COMPARTMENT D!
...SHE CAME TO THIS CAR YESTERDAY AND HASN'T BEEN SEEN SINCE!
SHE CAME TO FIND OUT IF IT WAS TRUE THAT A GUY FROM THE TAIL WAS *CAPTURED...*
OKAY. GO BACK TO YOUR COMPARTMENTS. I'LL CLEAR THIS UP WITH THE LIEUTENANT.
FREE OUR COMRADE! END THE ROLLING GHETTOS!
WHAT'S ALL THIS ABOUT, THEN? WHY ARE YOU DETAINING THIS WOMAN?
OH, DON'T WORRY. WE HAVEN'T HARMED HER, I ASSURE YOU. SHE COMMITTED AN OFFENCE: WE'RE DETAINING HER FOR QUESTIONING, THAT'S ALL.
AND THESE ACCUSATIONS OF A CAPTURED TAIL-RAT? YOU WANT TO STOP THE GIRL FROM *TALKING,* IS THAT IT?
YOU SHOULDN'T BELIEVE *ALL* OF THE NONSENSE YOU HEAR FROM THESE TAIL-RAT-LOVERS...
FAIR ENOUGH. BUT THEN... I'M SURE YOU WON'T HAVE ANY OBJECTIONS IF I PAY HER A VISIT? AS A REPRESENTATIVE OF THE CIVIL AUTHORITY, I MUST MAKE SURE THAT--
SORRY... BUT THE CIVIL AUTHORITY HAS NO JURISDICTION HERE.
YOU'RE ON MILITARY TERRITORY; MY AUTHORITY PREVAILS. THE DETAINEE WILL BE FREED WHEN THE TIME IS RIGHT, AND, IN THE MEANTIME, NO STRANGER TO THIS CARRIAGE WILL BE ALLOWED TO SEE HER. IS THAT CLEAR?
FINE -- IF THAT'S HOW YOU WANT TO PLAY IT... BUT I WARN YOU... I'LL HAVE TO REPORT THIS.

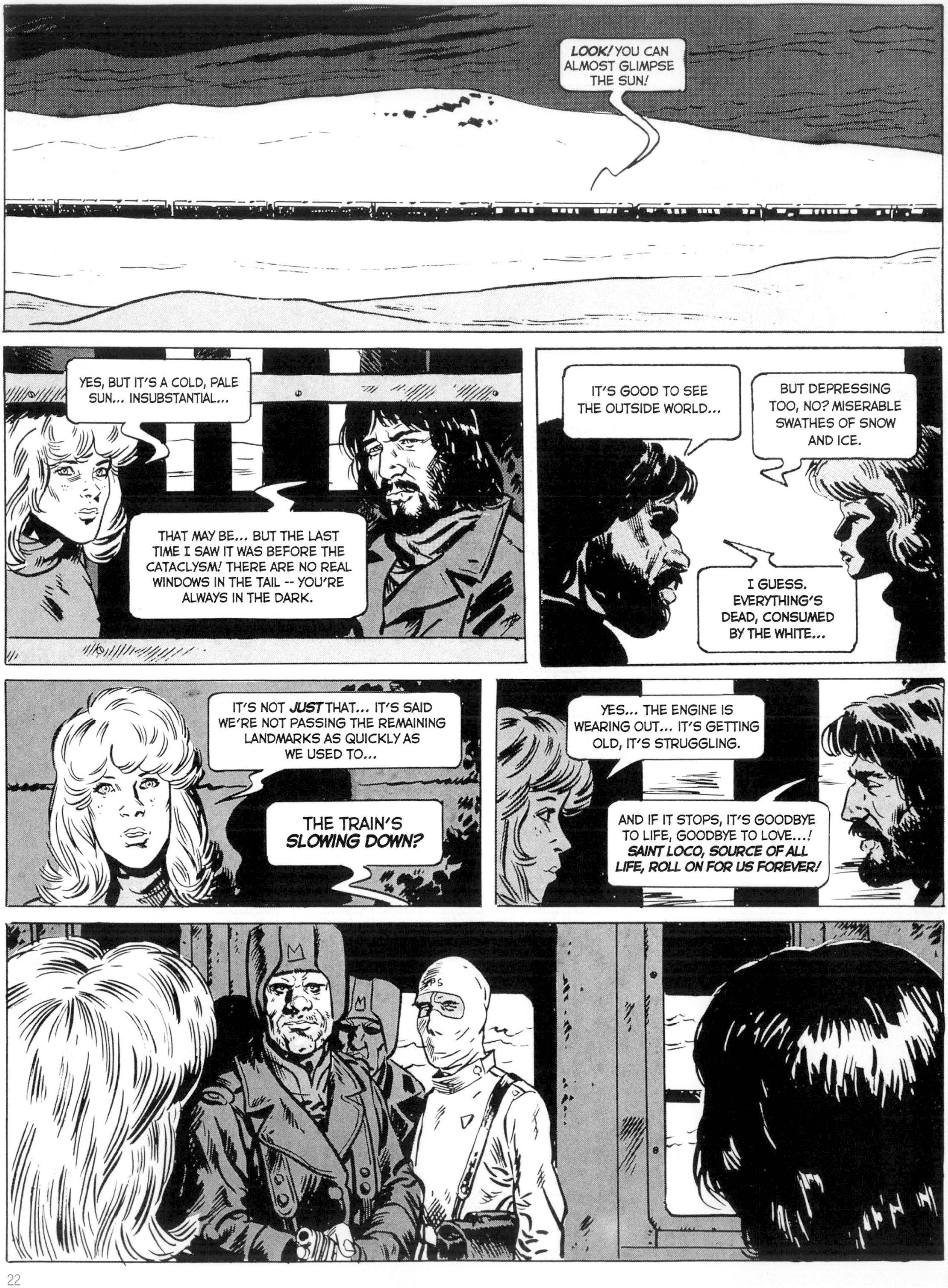
LOOK! YOU CAN ALMOST GLIMPSE THE SUN!
YES, BUT IT'S A COLD, PALE SUN... INSUBSTANTIAL...
THAT MAY BE... BUT THE LAST TIME I SAW IT WAS BEFORE THE CATACLYSM! THERE ARE NO REAL WINDOWS IN THE TAIL -- YOU'RE ALWAYS IN THE DARK.
IT'S GOOD TO SEE THE OUTSIDE WORLD...
BUT DEPRESSING TOO, NO? MISERABLE SWATHES OF SNOW AND ICE.
I GUESS. EVERYTHING'S DEAD, CONSUMED BY THE WHITE...
IT'S NOT JUST THAT... IT'S SAID WE'RE NOT PASSING THE REMAINING LANDMARKS AS QUICKLY AS WE USED TO...
THE TRAIN'S SLOWING DOWN?
YES... THE ENGINE IS WEARING OUT... IT'S GETTING OLD, IT'S STRUGGLING.
AND IF IT STOPS, IT'S GOODBYE TO LIFE, GOODBYE TO LOVE...! SAINT LOCO, SOURCE OF ALL LIFE, ROLL ON FOR US FOREVER!

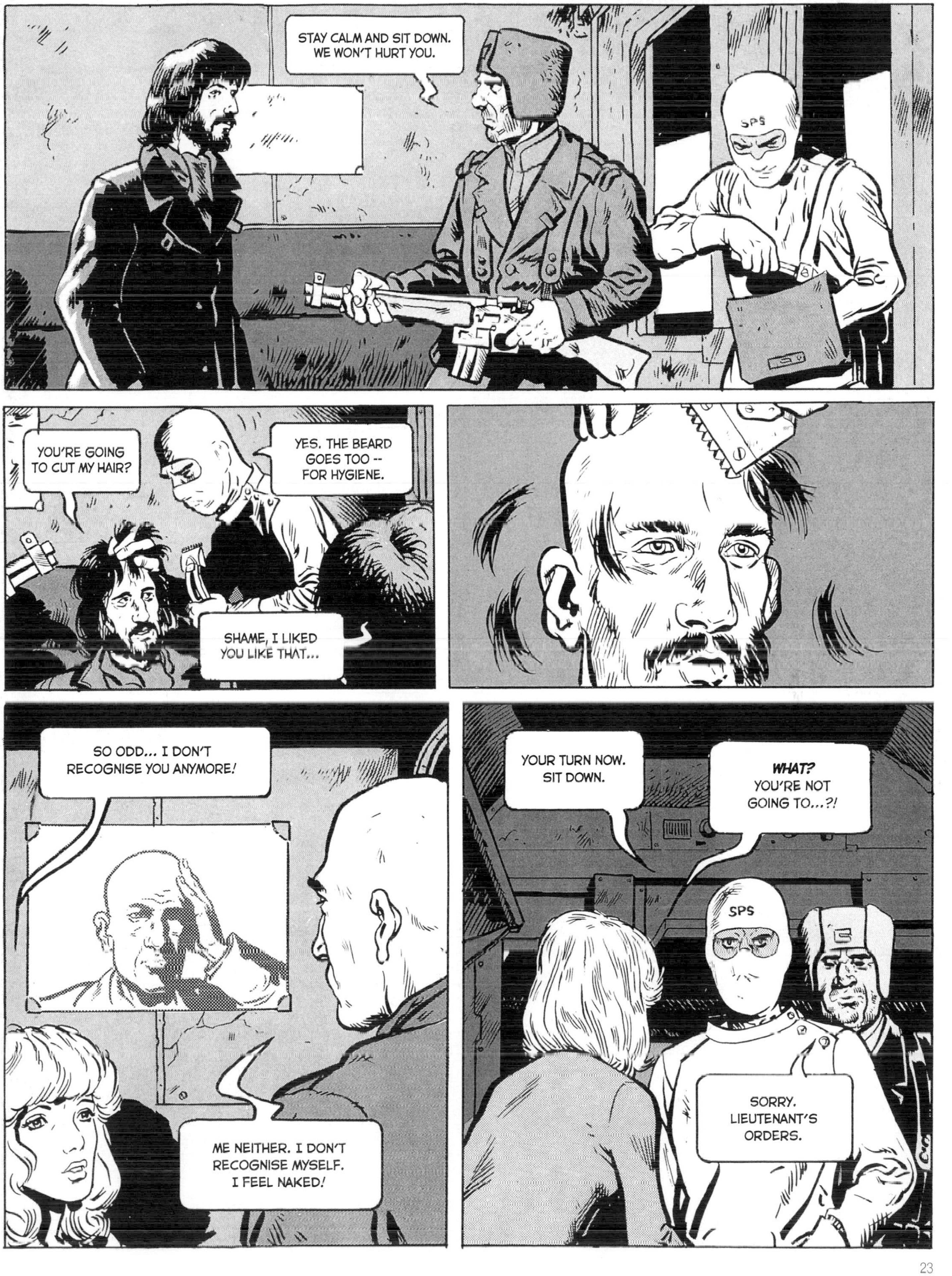

STAY CALM AND SIT DOWN. WE WON'T HURT YOU.
SPS
YOU'RE GOING TO CUT MY HAIR?
YES. THE BEARD GOES TOO -- FOR HYGIENE.
SHAME, I LIKED YOU LIKE THAT...
SO ODD... I DON'T RECOGNISE YOU ANYMORE!
ME NEITHER. I DON'T RECOGNISE MYSELF. I FEEL NAKED!
YOUR TURN NOW. SIT DOWN.
WHAT? YOU'RE NOT GOING TO...?!
SPS
SORRY. LIEUTENANT'S ORDERS.

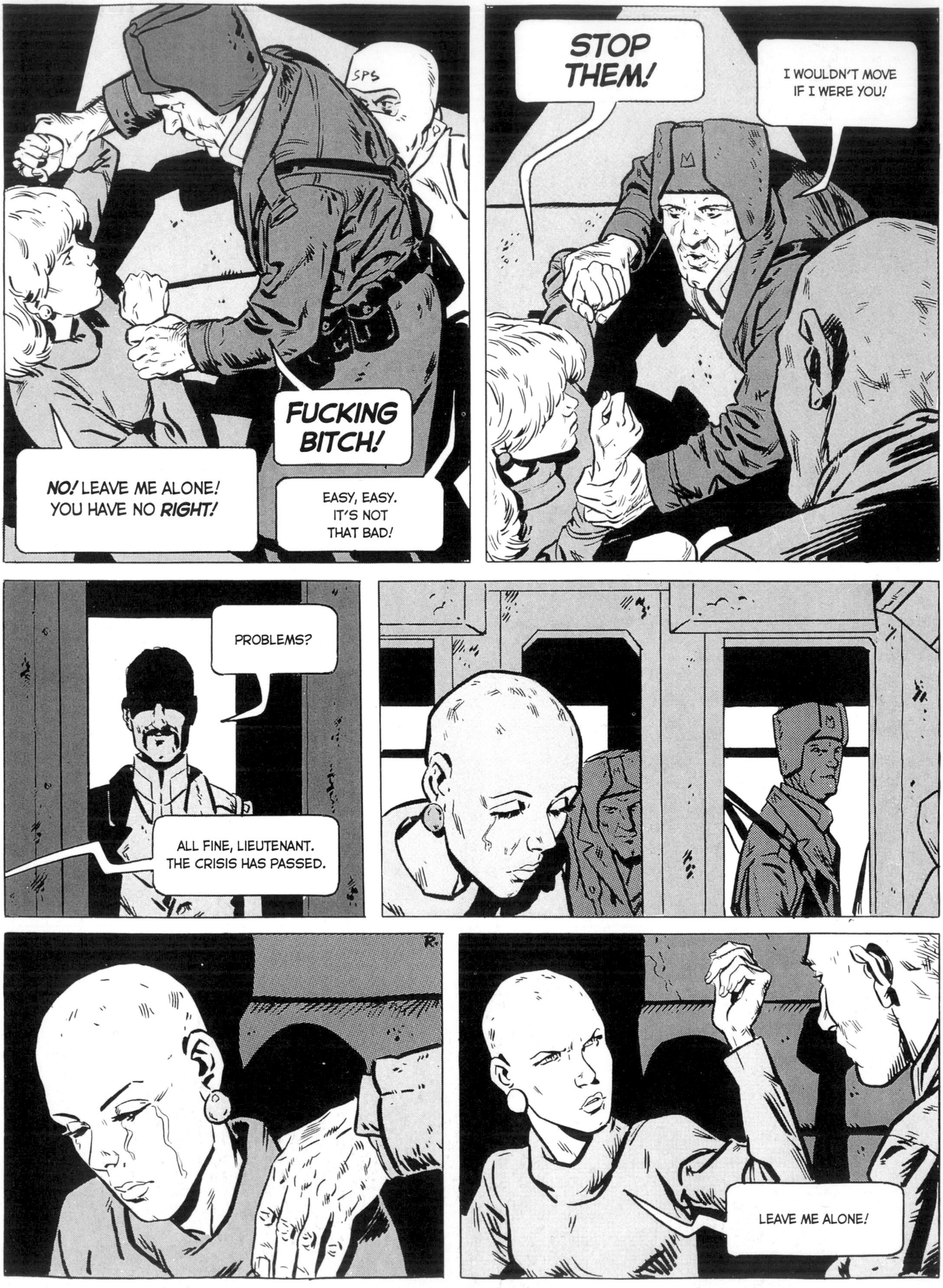
FUCKING BITCH!
NO! LEAVE ME ALONE! YOU HAVE NO RIGHT!
EASY, EASY. IT'S NOT THAT BAD!
STOP THEM!
I WOULDN'T MOVE IF I WERE YOU!
PROBLEMS?
ALL FINE, LIEUTENANT. THE CRISIS HAS PASSED.
LEAVE ME ALONE!

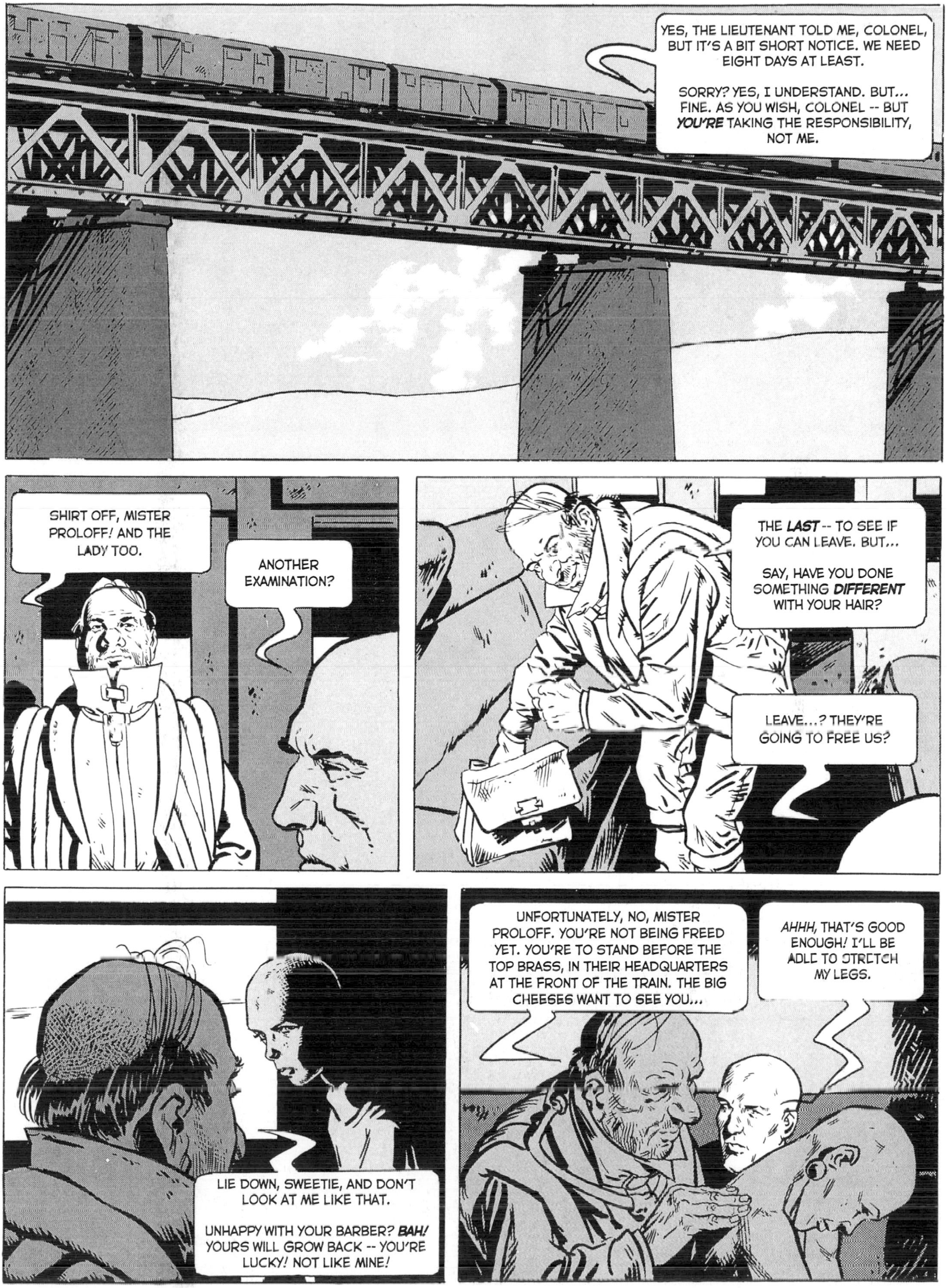
YES, THE LIEUTENANT TOLD ME, COLONEL, BUT IT'S A BIT SHORT NOTICE. WE NEED EIGHT DAYS AT LEAST.
SORRY? YES, I UNDERSTAND. BUT... FINE. AS YOU WISH, COLONEL -- BUT YOU'RE TAKING THE RESPONSIBILITY, NOT ME.
SHIRT OFF, MISTER PROLOFF! AND THE LADY TOO.
ANOTHER EXAMINATION?
THE LAST -- TO SEE IF YOU CAN LEAVE. BUT...
SAY, HAVE YOU DONE SOMETHING DIFFERENT WITH YOUR HAIR?
LEAVE...? THEY'RE GOING TO FREE US?
LIE DOWN, SWEETIE, AND DON'T LOOK AT ME LIKE THAT.
UNHAPPY WITH YOUR BARBER? BAH! YOURS WILL GROW BACK -- YOU'RE LUCKY! NOT LIKE MINE!
UNFORTUNATELY, NO, MISTER PROLOFF. YOU'RE NOT BEING FREED YET. YOU'RE TO STAND BEFORE THE TOP BRASS, IN THEIR HEADQUARTERS AT THE FRONT OF THE TRAIN. THE BIG CHEESES WANT TO SEE YOU...
AHHH, THAT'S GOOD ENOUGH! I'LL BE ABLE TO STRETCH MY LEGS.

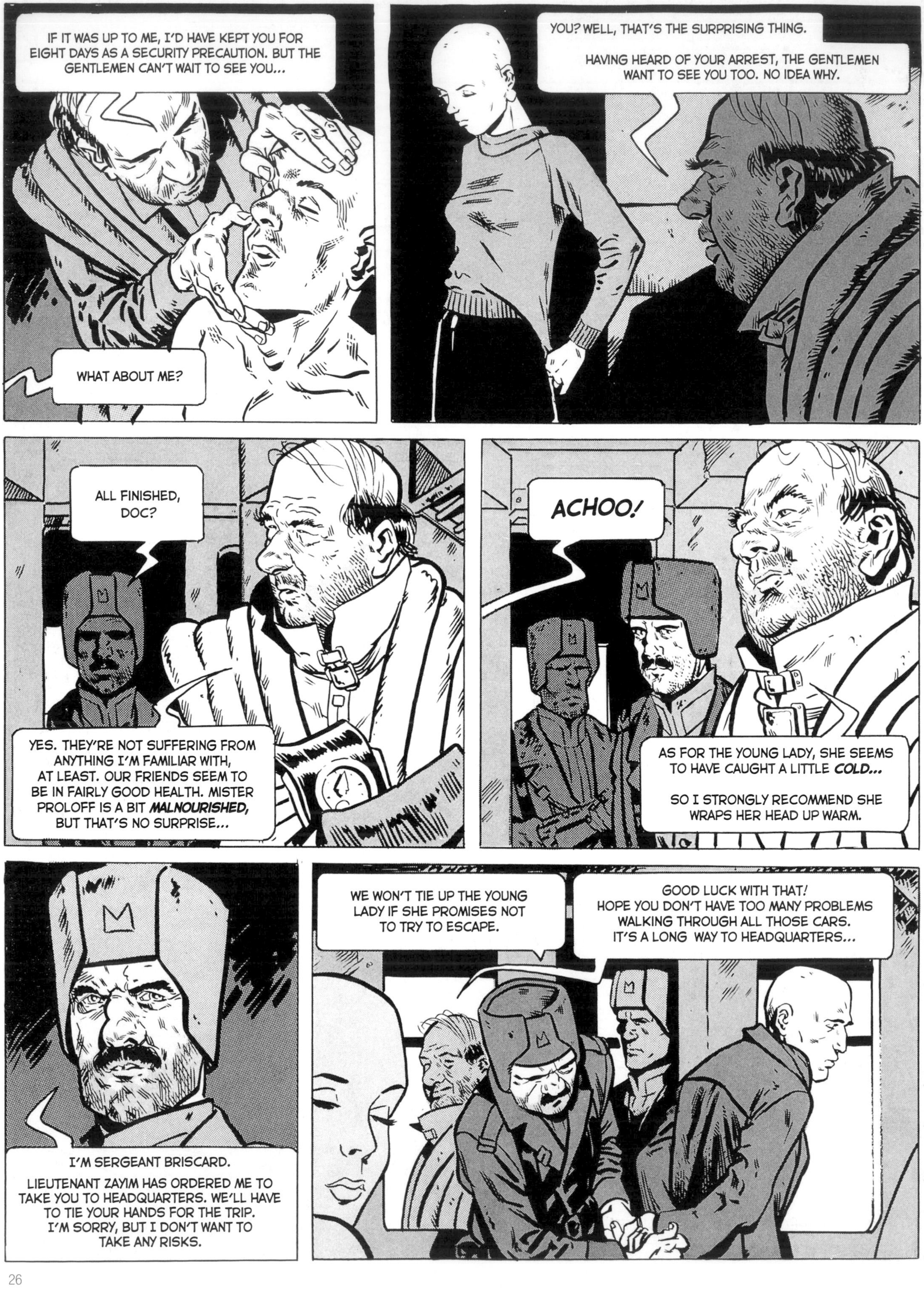
IF IT WAS UP TO ME, I'D HAVE KEPT YOU FOR EIGHT DAYS AS A SECURITY PRECAUTION. BUT THE GENTLEMEN CAN'T WAIT TO SEE YOU...
WHAT ABOUT ME?
YOU? WELL, THAT'S THE SURPRISING THING.
HAVING HEARD OF YOUR ARREST, THE GENTLEMEN WANT TO SEE YOU TOO. NO IDEA WHY.
ALL FINISHED, DOC?
YES. THEY'RE NOT SUFFERING FROM ANYTHING I'M FAMILIAR WITH, AT LEAST. OUR FRIENDS SEEM TO BE IN FAIRLY GOOD HEALTH. MISTER PROLOFF IS A BIT MALNOURISHED, BUT THAT'S NO SURPRISE...
ACHOO!
AS FOR THE YOUNG LADY, SHE SEEMS TO HAVE CAUGHT A LITTLE COLD...
SO I STRONGLY RECOMMEND SHE WRAPS HER HEAD UP WARM.
I'M SERGEANT BRISCARD.
LIEUTENANT ZAYIM HAS ORDERED ME TO TAKE YOU TO HEADQUARTERS. WE'LL HAVE TO TIE YOUR HANDS FOR THE TRIP. I'M SORRY, BUT I DON'T WANT TO TAKE ANY RISKS.
WE WON'T TIE UP THE YOUNG LADY IF SHE PROMISES NOT TO TRY TO ESCAPE.
GOOD LUCK WITH THAT! HOPE YOU DON'T HAVE TOO MANY PROBLEMS WALKING THROUGH ALL THOSE CARS. IT'S A LONG WAY TO HEADQUARTERS...

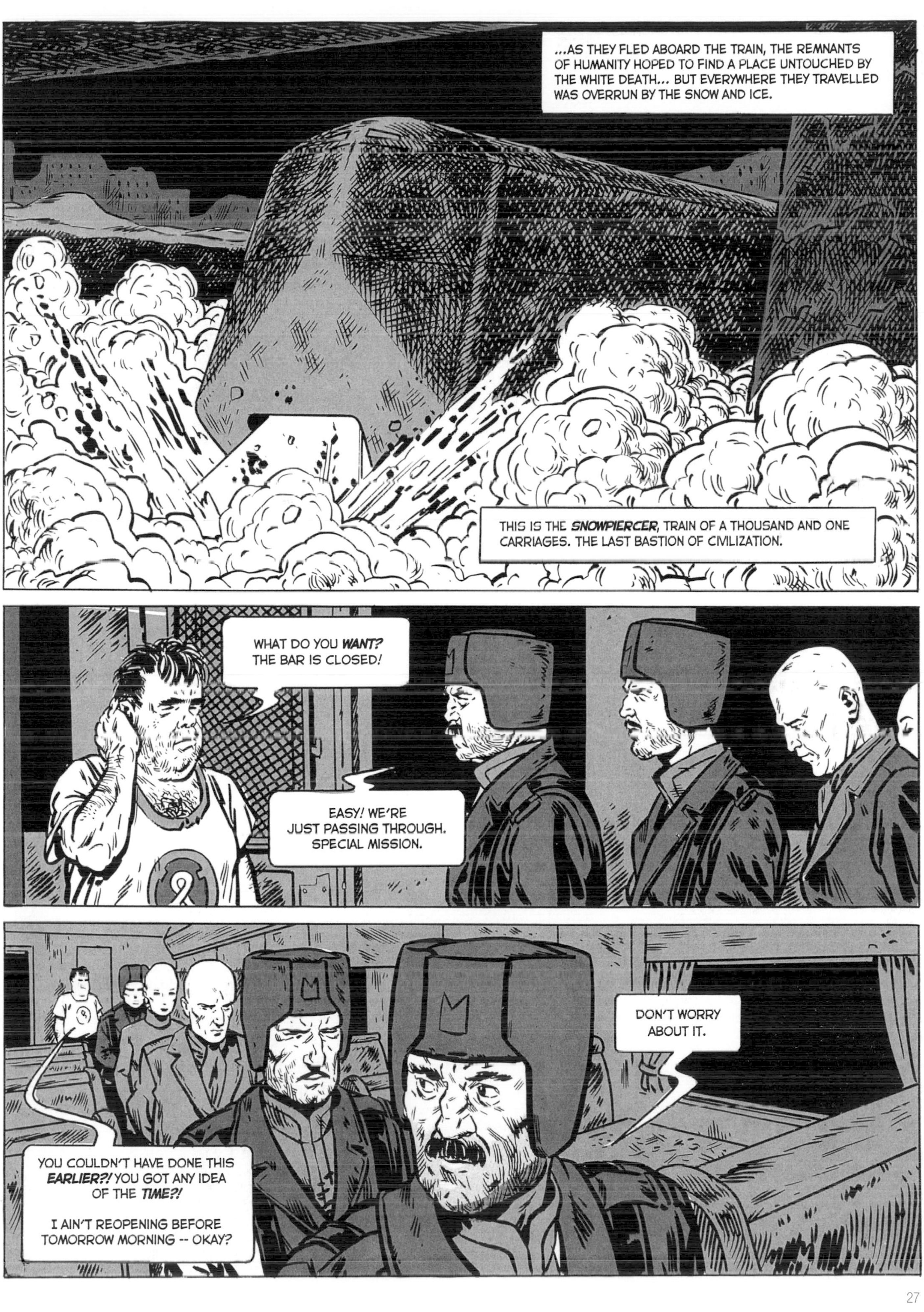
...AS THEY FLED ABOARD THE TRAIN, THE REMNANTS OF HUMANITY HOPED TO FIND A PLACE UNTOUCHED BY THE WHITE DEATH... BUT EVERYWHERE THEY TRAVELLED WAS OVERRUN BY THE SNOW AND ICE.
THIS IS THE *SNOWPIERCER*, TRAIN OF A THOUSAND AND ONE CARRIAGES. THE LAST BASTION OF CIVILIZATION.
WHAT DO YOU *WANT?* THE BAR IS CLOSED!
EASY! WE'RE JUST PASSING THROUGH. SPECIAL MISSION.
DON'T WORRY ABOUT IT.
YOU COULDN'T HAVE DONE THIS *EARLIER?!* YOU GOT ANY IDEA OF THE *TIME?!*
I AIN'T REOPENING BEFORE TOMORROW MORNING -- OKAY?

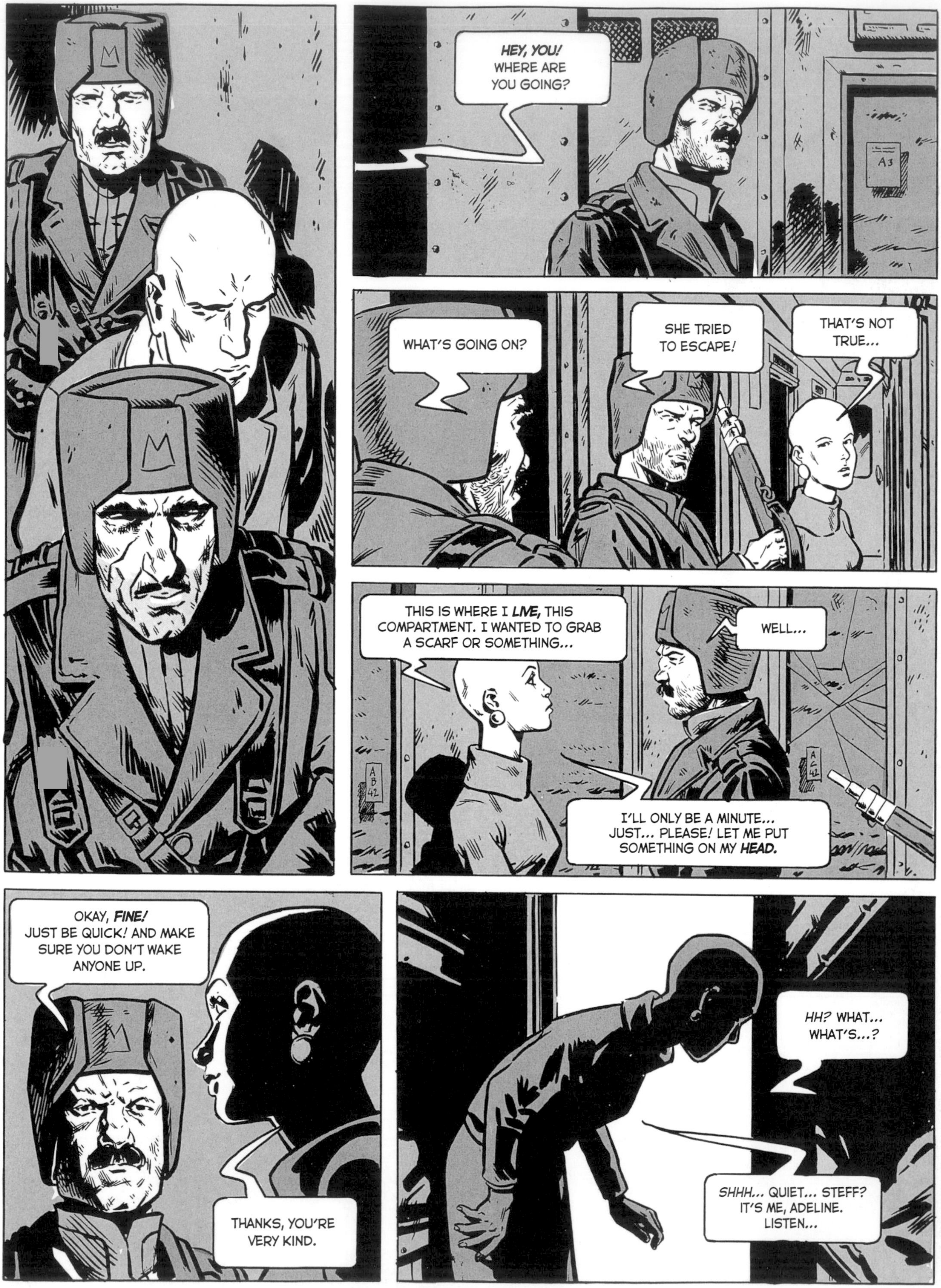
HEY, YOU! WHERE ARE YOU GOING?
WHAT'S GOING ON?
SHE TRIED TO ESCAPE!
THAT'S NOT TRUE...
A3
THIS IS WHERE I LIVE, THIS COMPARTMENT. I WANTED TO GRAB A SCARF OR SOMETHING...
WELL...
AB 42
AC 42
I'LL ONLY BE A MINUTE... JUST... PLEASE! LET ME PUT SOMETHING ON MY HEAD.
OKAY, FINE! JUST BE QUICK! AND MAKE SURE YOU DON'T WAKE ANYONE UP.
THANKS, YOU'RE VERY KIND.
HH? WHAT... WHAT'S...?
SHHH... QUIET... STEFF? IT'S ME, ADELINE. LISTEN...

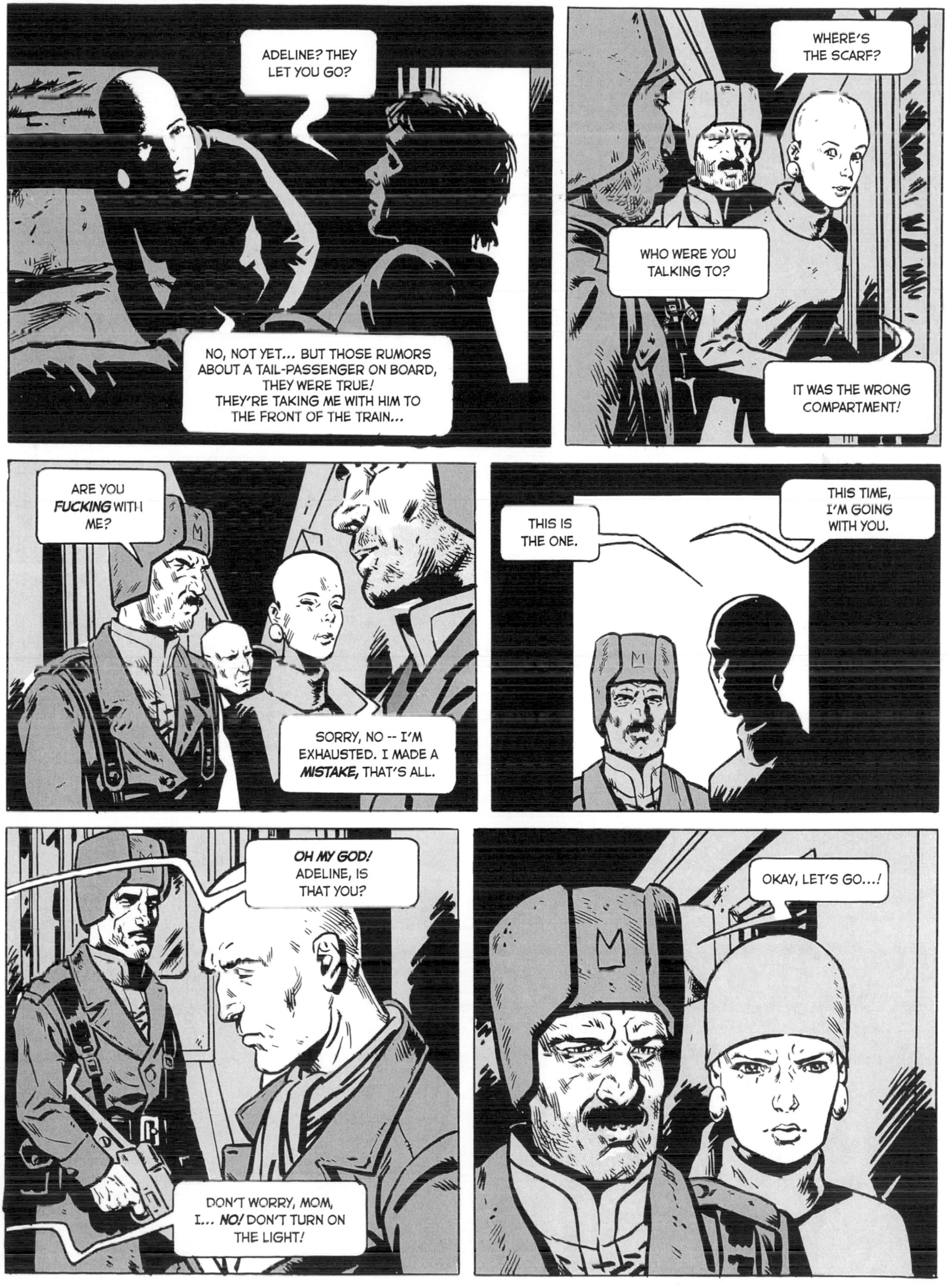
ADELINE? THEY LET YOU GO?
NO, NOT YET... BUT THOSE RUMORS ABOUT A TAIL-PASSENGER ON BOARD, THEY WERE TRUE! THEY'RE TAKING ME WITH HIM TO THE FRONT OF THE TRAIN...
WHERE'S THE SCARF?
WHO WERE YOU TALKING TO?
IT WAS THE WRONG COMPARTMENT!
ARE YOU FUCKING WITH ME?
SORRY, NO -- I'M EXHAUSTED. I MADE A MISTAKE, THAT'S ALL.
THIS IS THE ONE.
THIS TIME, I'M GOING WITH YOU.
OH MY GOD! ADELINE, IS THAT YOU?
DON'T WORRY, MOM, I... NO! DON'T TURN ON THE LIGHT!
OKAY, LET'S GO...!

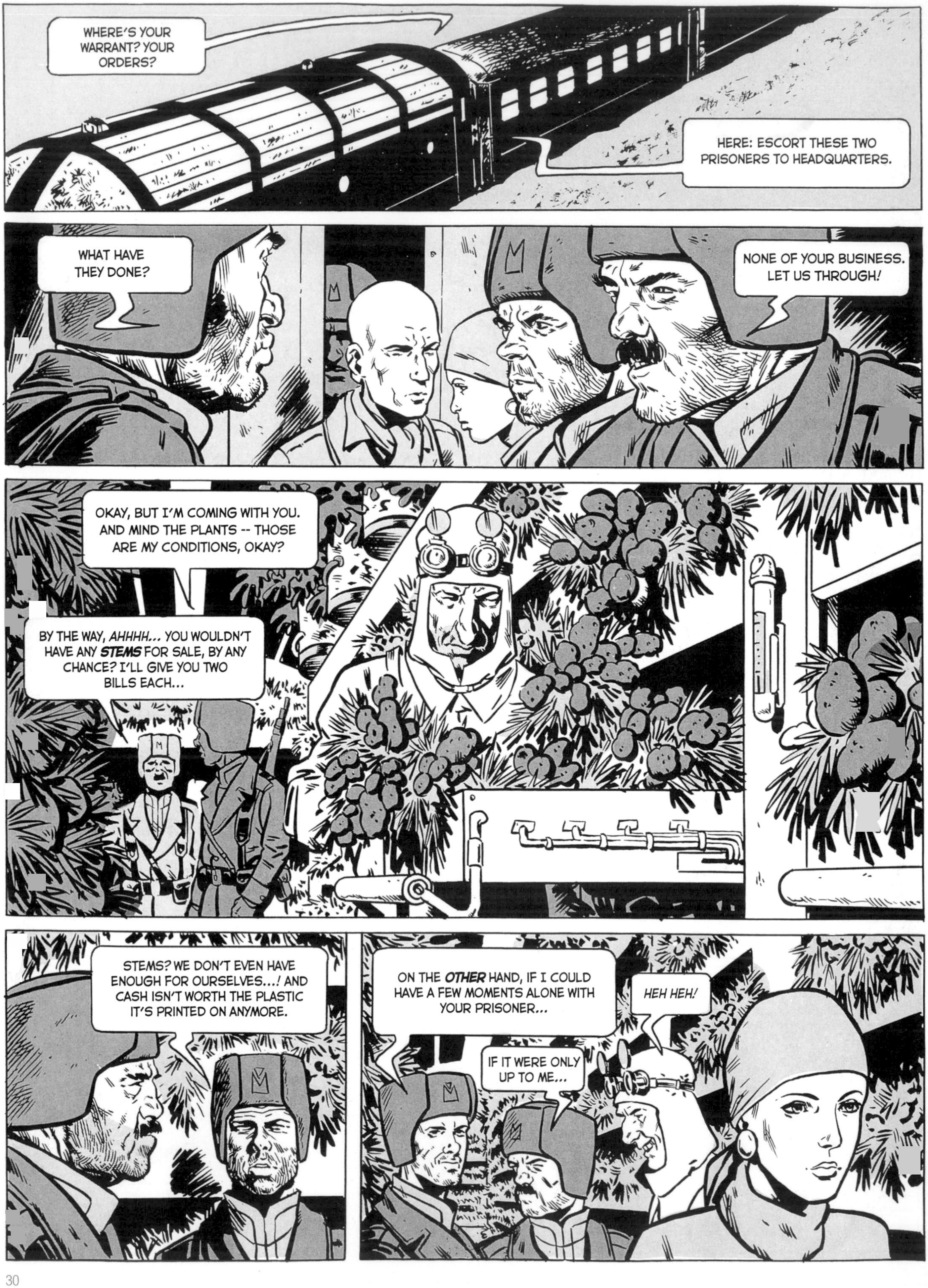
WHERE'S YOUR WARRANT? YOUR ORDERS?
HERE: ESCORT THESE TWO PRISONERS TO HEADQUARTERS.
WHAT HAVE THEY DONE?
NONE OF YOUR BUSINESS. LET US THROUGH!
OKAY, BUT I'M COMING WITH YOU. AND MIND THE PLANTS -- THOSE ARE MY CONDITIONS, OKAY?
BY THE WAY, *AHHHH...* YOU WOULDN'T HAVE ANY ***STEMS*** FOR SALE, BY ANY CHANCE? I'LL GIVE YOU TWO BILLS EACH...
STEMS? WE DON'T EVEN HAVE ENOUGH FOR OURSELVES...! AND CASH ISN'T WORTH THE PLASTIC IT'S PRINTED ON ANYMORE.
ON THE ***OTHER*** HAND, IF I COULD HAVE A FEW MOMENTS ALONE WITH YOUR PRISONER...
HEH HEH!
IF IT WERE ONLY UP TO ME...

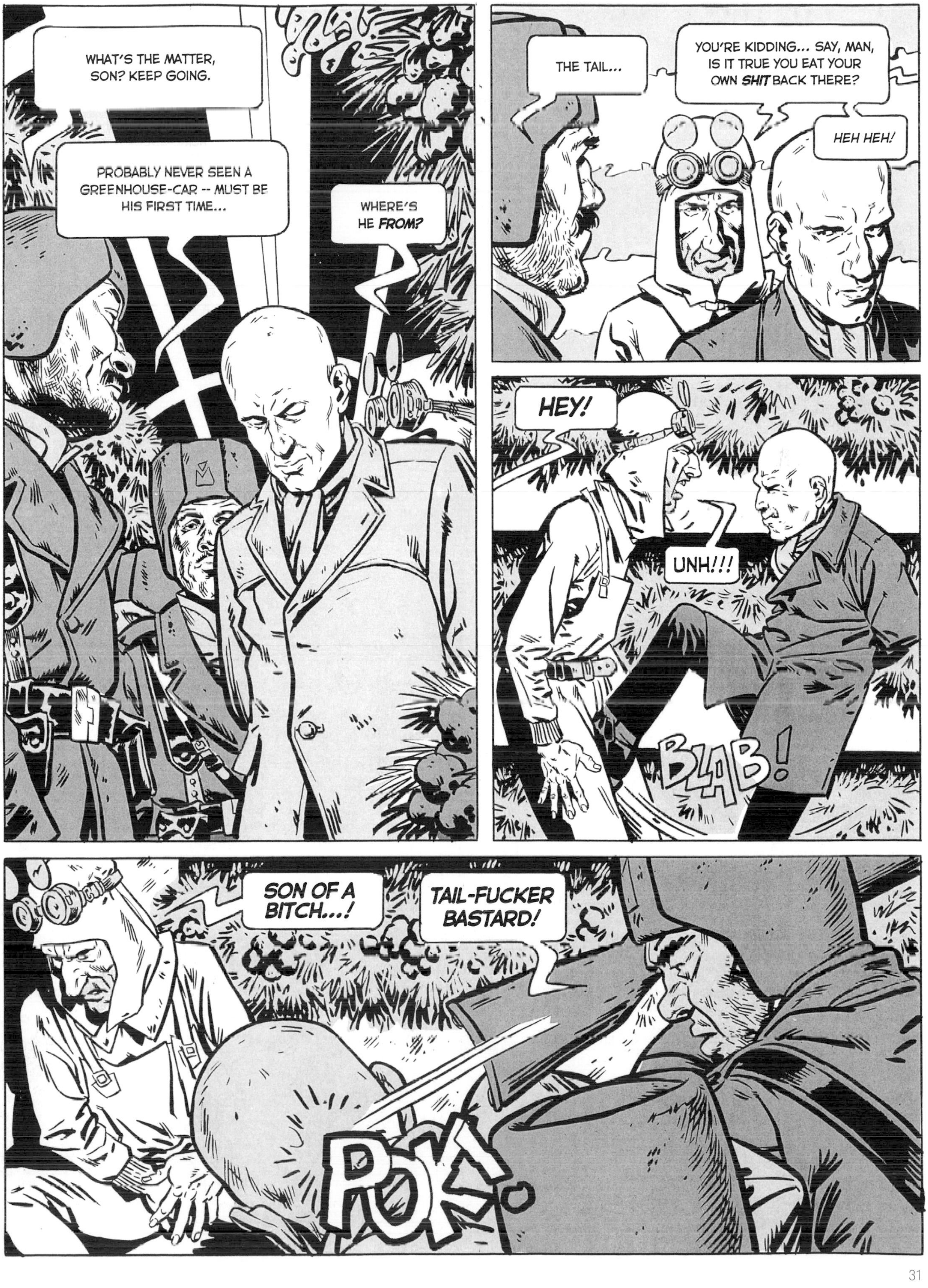
WHAT'S THE MATTER, SON? KEEP GOING.
PROBABLY NEVER SEEN A GREENHOUSE-CAR -- MUST BE HIS FIRST TIME...
WHERE'S HE FROM?
THE TAIL...
YOU'RE KIDDING... SAY, MAN, IS IT TRUE YOU EAT YOUR OWN SHIT BACK THERE?
HEH HEH!
HEY!
UNH!!!
BLAB!
SON OF A BITCH...!
TAIL-FUCKER BASTARD!
POK.

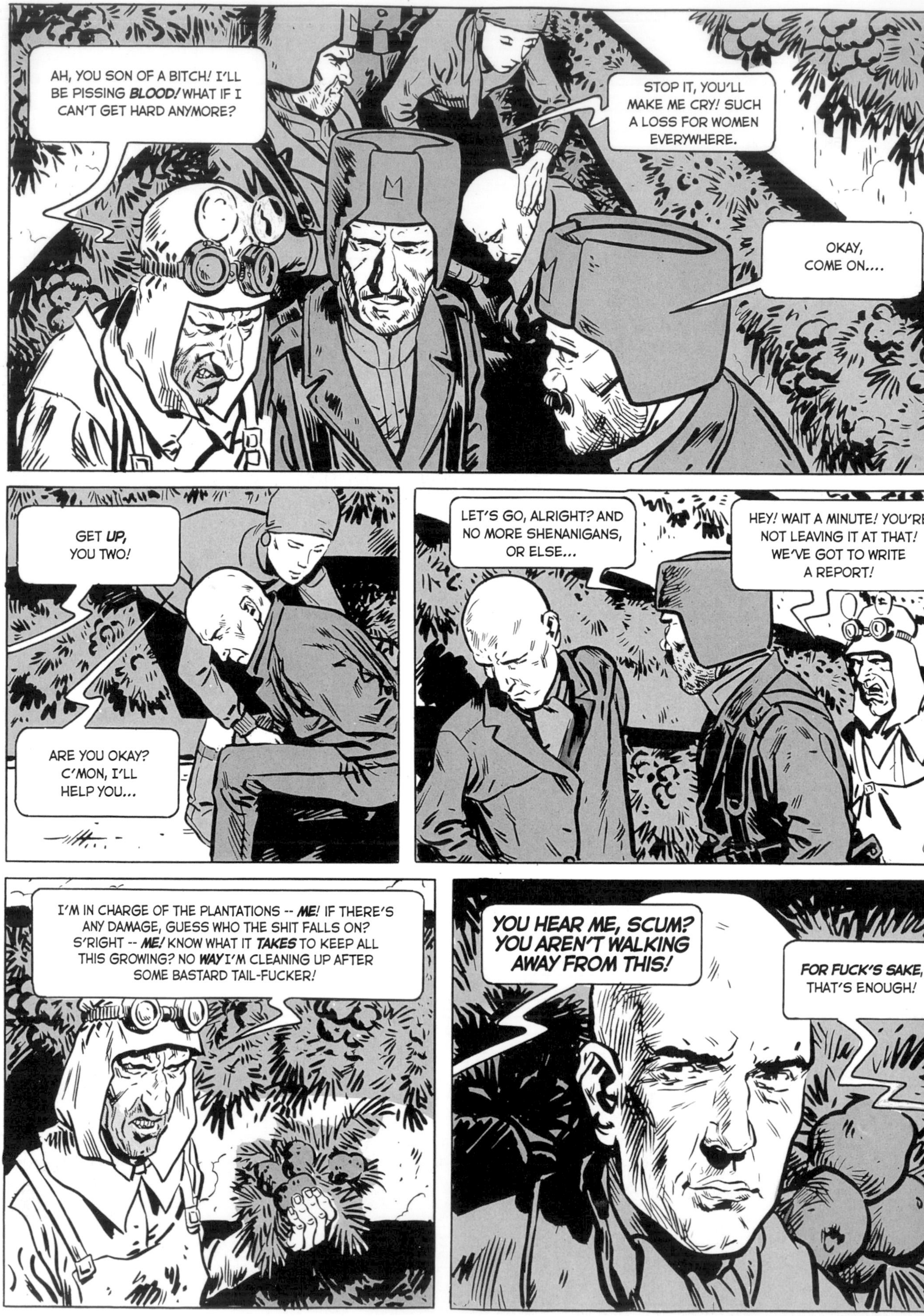
AH, YOU SON OF A BITCH! I'LL BE PISSING BLOOD! WHAT IF I CAN'T GET HARD ANYMORE?
STOP IT, YOU'LL MAKE ME CRY! SUCH A LOSS FOR WOMEN EVERYWHERE.
OKAY, COME ON....
GET UP, YOU TWO!
ARE YOU OKAY? C'MON, I'LL HELP YOU...
LET'S GO, ALRIGHT? AND NO MORE SHENANIGANS, OR ELSE...
HEY! WAIT A MINUTE! YOU'RE NOT LEAVING IT AT THAT! WE'VE GOT TO WRITE A REPORT!
I'M IN CHARGE OF THE PLANTATIONS -- ME! IF THERE'S ANY DAMAGE, GUESS WHO THE SHIT FALLS ON? S'RIGHT -- ME! KNOW WHAT IT TAKES TO KEEP ALL THIS GROWING? NO WAY I'M CLEANING UP AFTER SOME BASTARD TAIL-FUCKER!
YOU HEAR ME, SCUM? YOU AREN'T WALKING AWAY FROM THIS!
FOR FUCK'S SAKE, THAT'S ENOUGH!

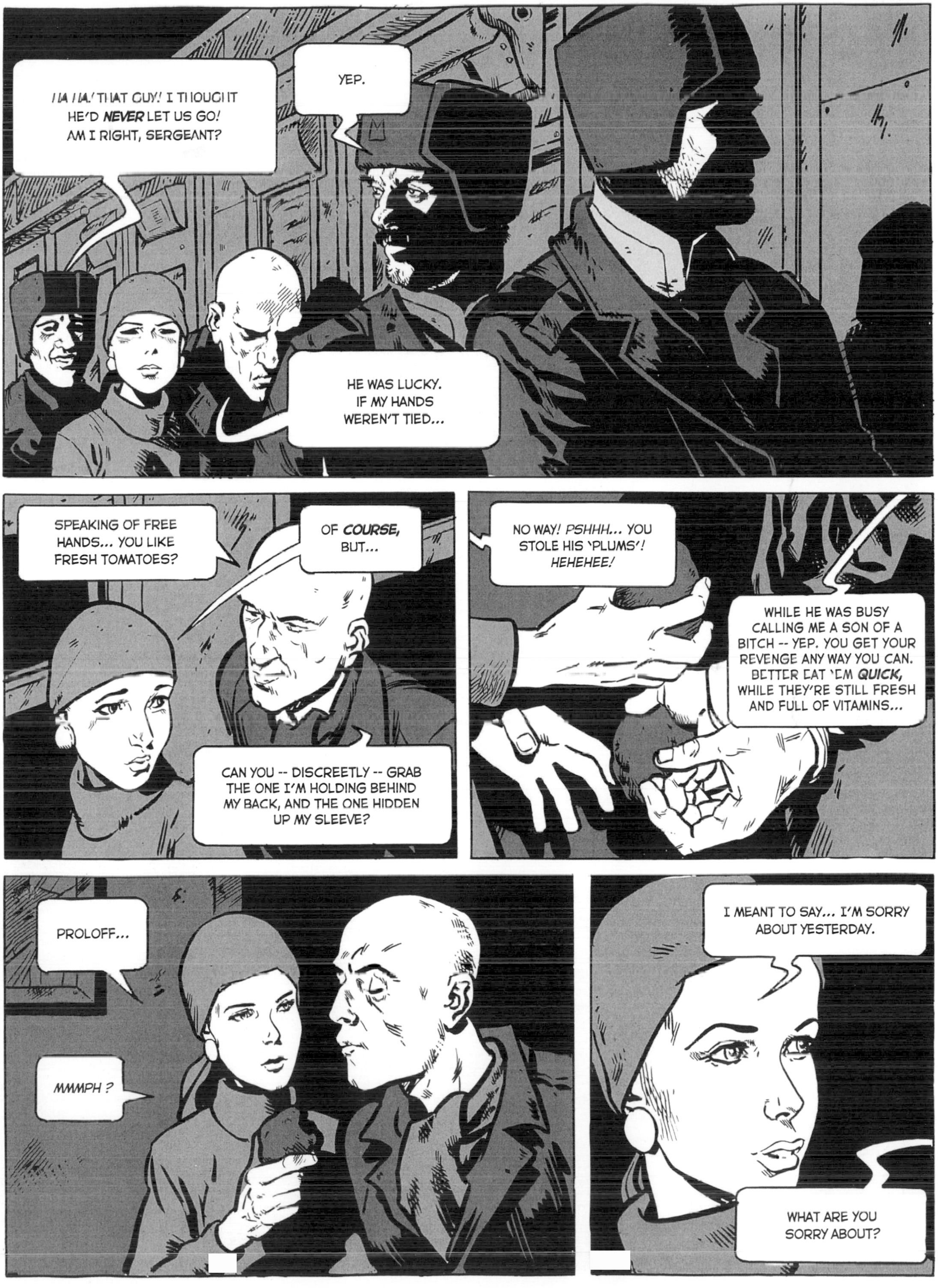
HA HA! THAT GUY! I THOUGHT HE'D NEVER LET US GO! AM I RIGHT, SERGEANT?
YEP.
HE WAS LUCKY. IF MY HANDS WEREN'T TIED...
SPEAKING OF FREE HANDS... YOU LIKE FRESH TOMATOES?
OF COURSE, BUT...
CAN YOU -- DISCREETLY -- GRAB THE ONE I'M HOLDING BEHIND MY BACK, AND THE ONE HIDDEN UP MY SLEEVE?
NO WAY! PSHHH... YOU STOLE HIS 'PLUMS'! HEHEHEE!
WHILE HE WAS BUSY CALLING ME A SON OF A BITCH -- YEP. YOU GET YOUR REVENGE ANY WAY YOU CAN. BETTER EAT 'EM QUICK, WHILE THEY'RE STILL FRESH AND FULL OF VITAMINS...
PROLOFF...
MMMPH ?
I MEANT TO SAY... I'M SORRY ABOUT YESTERDAY.
WHAT ARE YOU SORRY ABOUT?

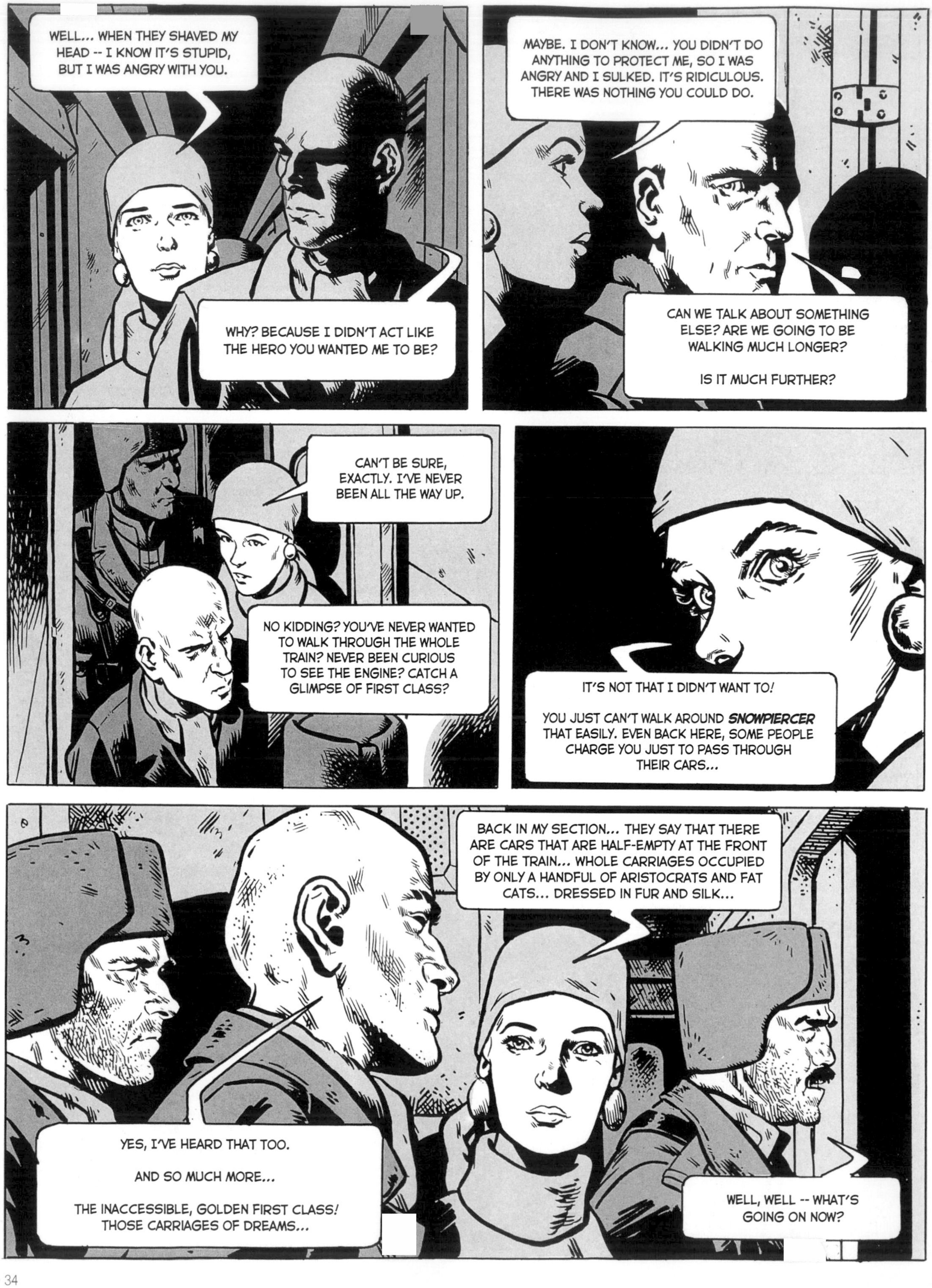
WELL... WHEN THEY SHAVED MY HEAD -- I KNOW IT'S STUPID, BUT I WAS ANGRY WITH YOU.
WHY? BECAUSE I DIDN'T ACT LIKE THE HERO YOU WANTED ME TO BE?
MAYBE. I DON'T KNOW... YOU DIDN'T DO ANYTHING TO PROTECT ME, SO I WAS ANGRY AND I SULKED. IT'S RIDICULOUS. THERE WAS NOTHING YOU COULD DO.
CAN WE TALK ABOUT SOMETHING ELSE? ARE WE GOING TO BE WALKING MUCH LONGER?
IS IT MUCH FURTHER?
CAN'T BE SURE, EXACTLY. I'VE NEVER BEEN ALL THE WAY UP.
NO KIDDING? YOU'VE NEVER WANTED TO WALK THROUGH THE WHOLE TRAIN? NEVER BEEN CURIOUS TO SEE THE ENGINE? CATCH A GLIMPSE OF FIRST CLASS?
IT'S NOT THAT I DIDN'T WANT TO!
YOU JUST CAN'T WALK AROUND ***SNOWPIERCER*** THAT EASILY. EVEN BACK HERE, SOME PEOPLE CHARGE YOU JUST TO PASS THROUGH THEIR CARS...
BACK IN MY SECTION... THEY SAY THAT THERE ARE CARS THAT ARE HALF-EMPTY AT THE FRONT OF THE TRAIN... WHOLE CARRIAGES OCCUPIED BY ONLY A HANDFUL OF ARISTOCRATS AND FAT CATS... DRESSED IN FUR AND SILK...
YES, I'VE HEARD THAT TOO.
AND SO MUCH MORE...
THE INACCESSIBLE, GOLDEN FIRST CLASS! THOSE CARRIAGES OF DREAMS...
WELL, WELL -- WHAT'S GOING ON NOW?

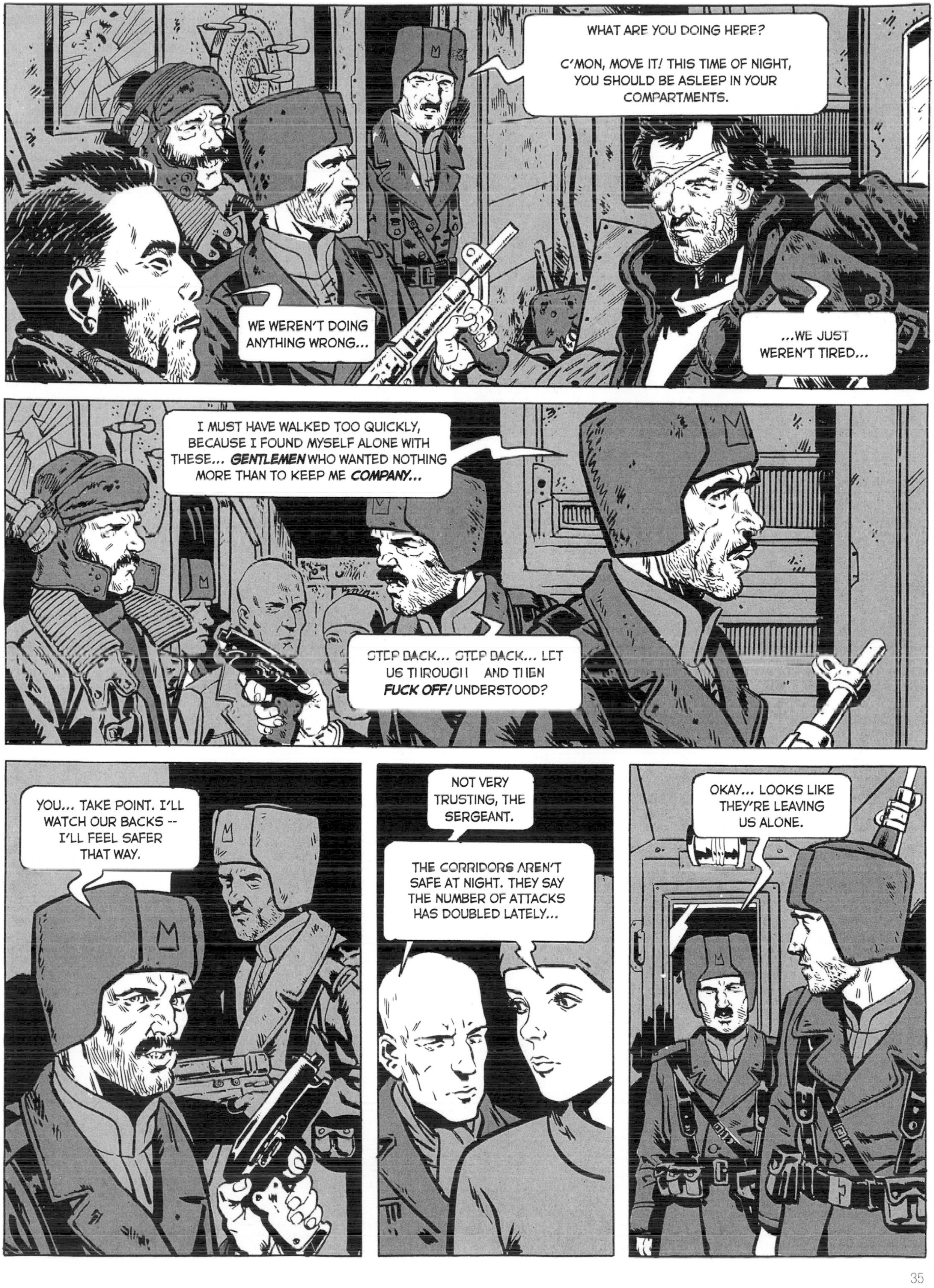
WHAT ARE YOU DOING HERE?
C'MON, MOVE IT! THIS TIME OF NIGHT, YOU SHOULD BE ASLEEP IN YOUR COMPARTMENTS.
WE WEREN'T DOING ANYTHING WRONG...
...WE JUST WEREN'T TIRED...
I MUST HAVE WALKED TOO QUICKLY, BECAUSE I FOUND MYSELF ALONE WITH THESE... GENTLEMEN WHO WANTED NOTHING MORE THAN TO KEEP ME COMPANY...
STEP BACK... STEP BACK... LET US THROUGH AND THEN FUCK OFF! UNDERSTOOD?
YOU... TAKE POINT. I'LL WATCH OUR BACKS -- I'LL FEEL SAFER THAT WAY.
NOT VERY TRUSTING, THE SERGEANT.
THE CORRIDORS AREN'T SAFE AT NIGHT. THEY SAY THE NUMBER OF ATTACKS HAS DOUBLED LATELY...
OKAY... LOOKS LIKE THEY'RE LEAVING US ALONE.

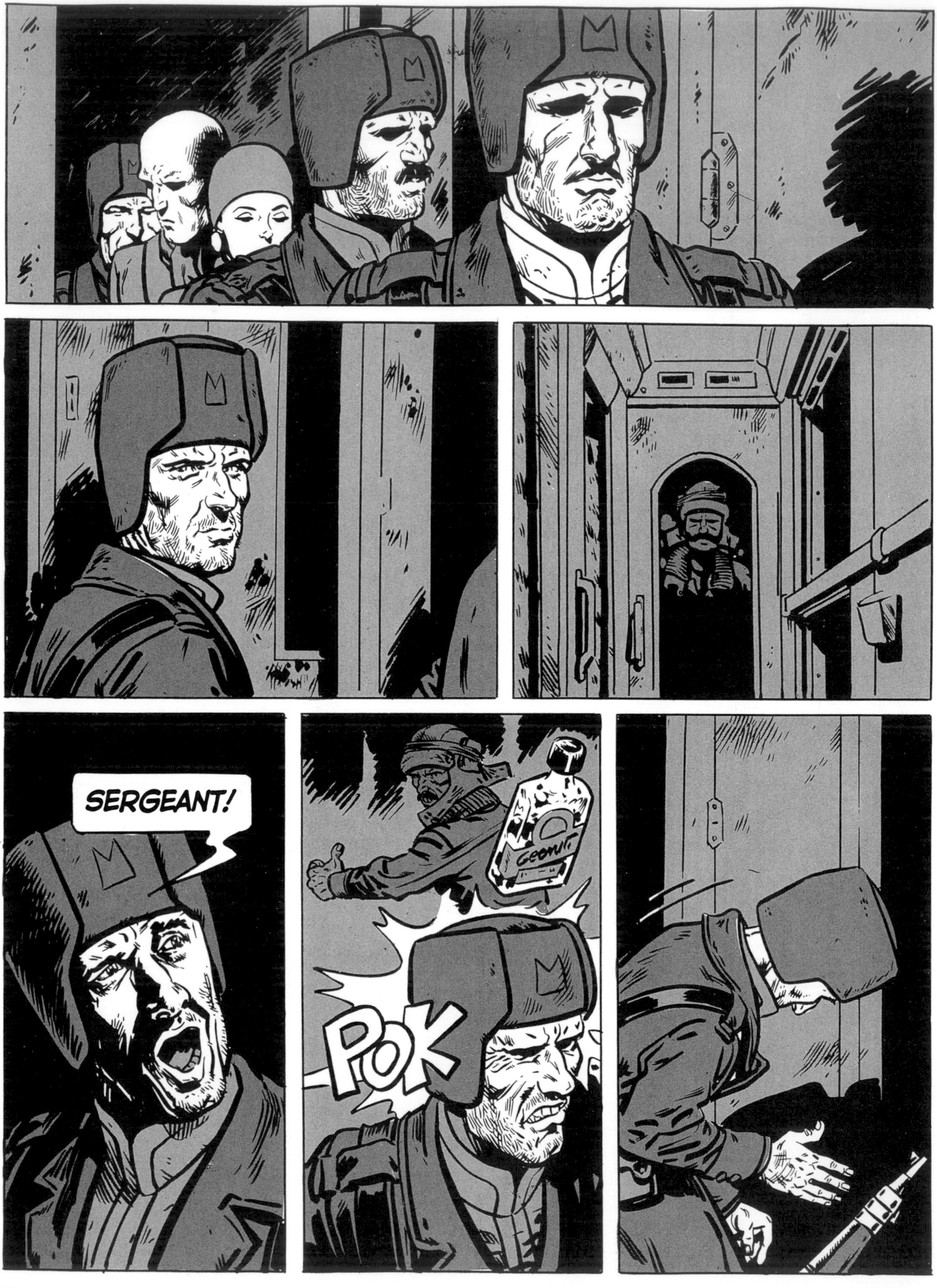
SERGEANT!
POK

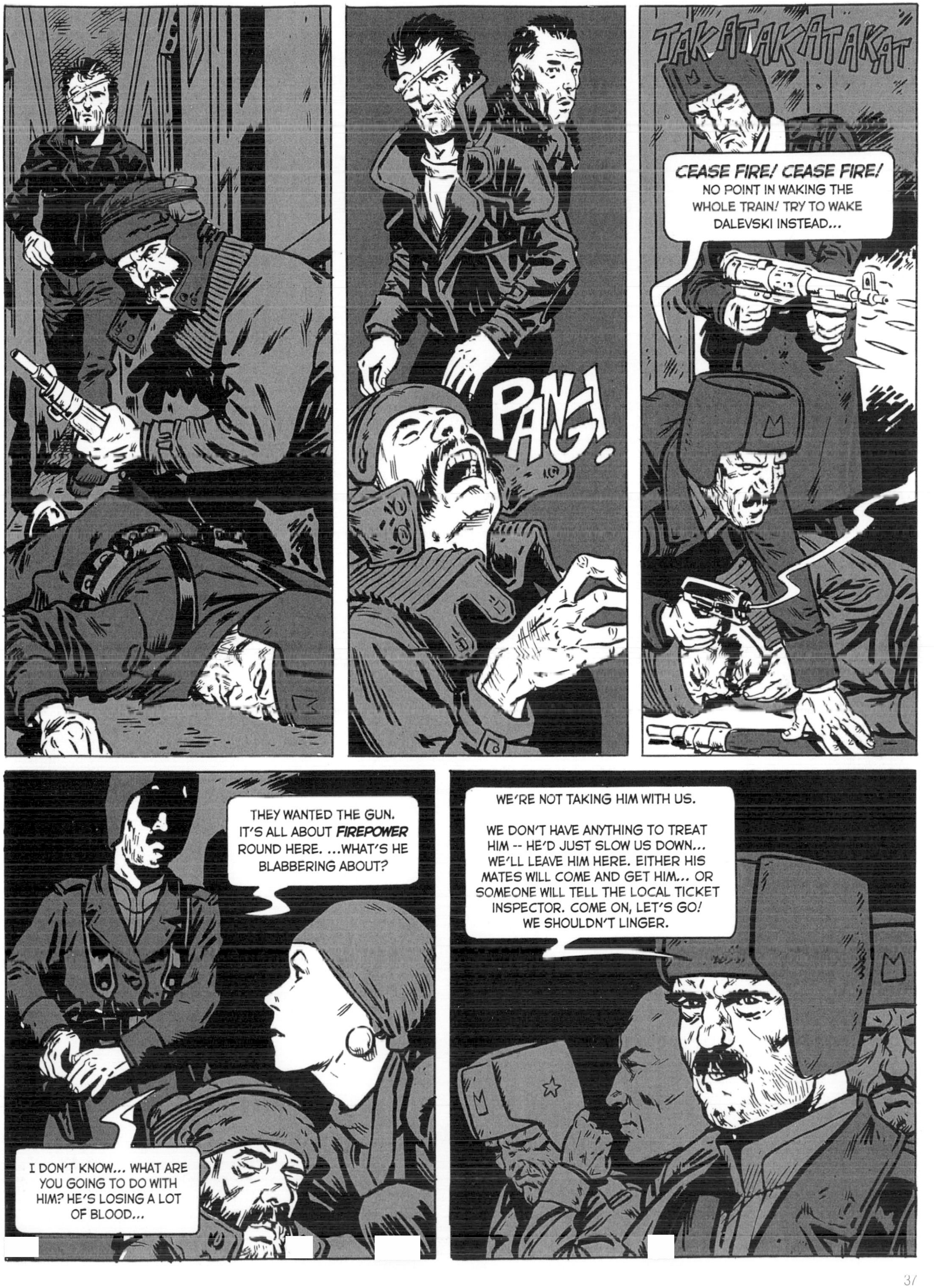
PANG!
TAKATAKATAKAT
CEASE FIRE! CEASE FIRE! NO POINT IN WAKING THE WHOLE TRAIN! TRY TO WAKE DALEVSKI INSTEAD...
THEY WANTED THE GUN. IT'S ALL ABOUT FIREPOWER ROUND HERE. ...WHAT'S HE BLABBERING ABOUT?
I DON'T KNOW... WHAT ARE YOU GOING TO DO WITH HIM? HE'S LOSING A LOT OF BLOOD...
WE'RE NOT TAKING HIM WITH US.
WE DON'T HAVE ANYTHING TO TREAT HIM -- HE'D JUST SLOW US DOWN... WE'LL LEAVE HIM HERE. EITHER HIS MATES WILL COME AND GET HIM... OR SOMEONE WILL TELL THE LOCAL TICKET INSPECTOR. COME ON, LET'S GO! WE SHOULDN'T LINGER.

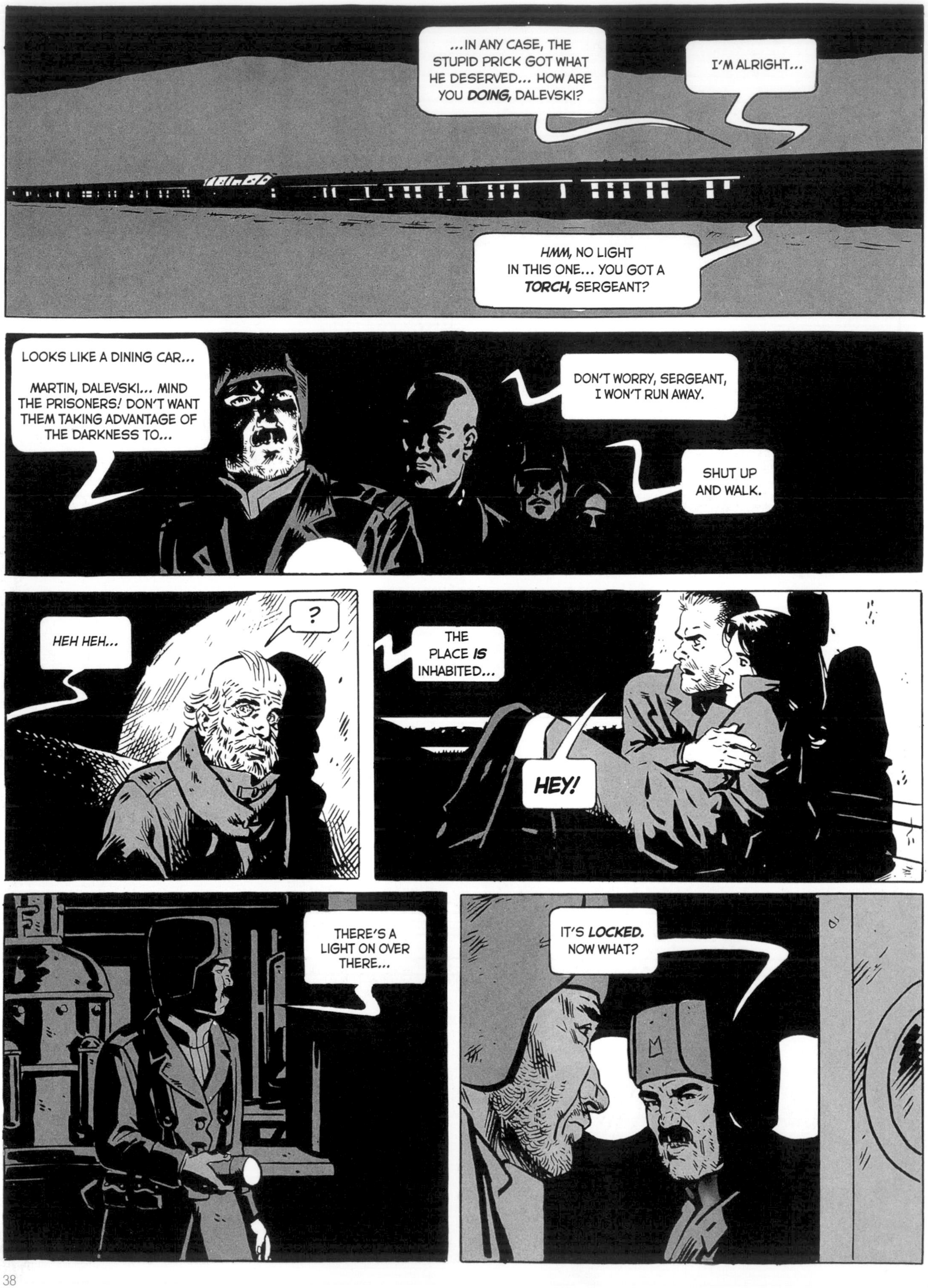
...IN ANY CASE, THE STUPID PRICK GOT WHAT HE DESERVED... HOW ARE YOU DOING, DALEVSKI?
I'M ALRIGHT...
HMM, NO LIGHT IN THIS ONE... YOU GOT A TORCH, SERGEANT?
LOOKS LIKE A DINING CAR...
MARTIN, DALEVSKI... MIND THE PRISONERS! DON'T WANT THEM TAKING ADVANTAGE OF THE DARKNESS TO...
DON'T WORRY, SERGEANT, I WON'T RUN AWAY.
SHUT UP AND WALK.
HEH HEH...
?
THE PLACE IS INHABITED...
HEY!
THERE'S A LIGHT ON OVER THERE...
IT'S LOCKED. NOW WHAT?

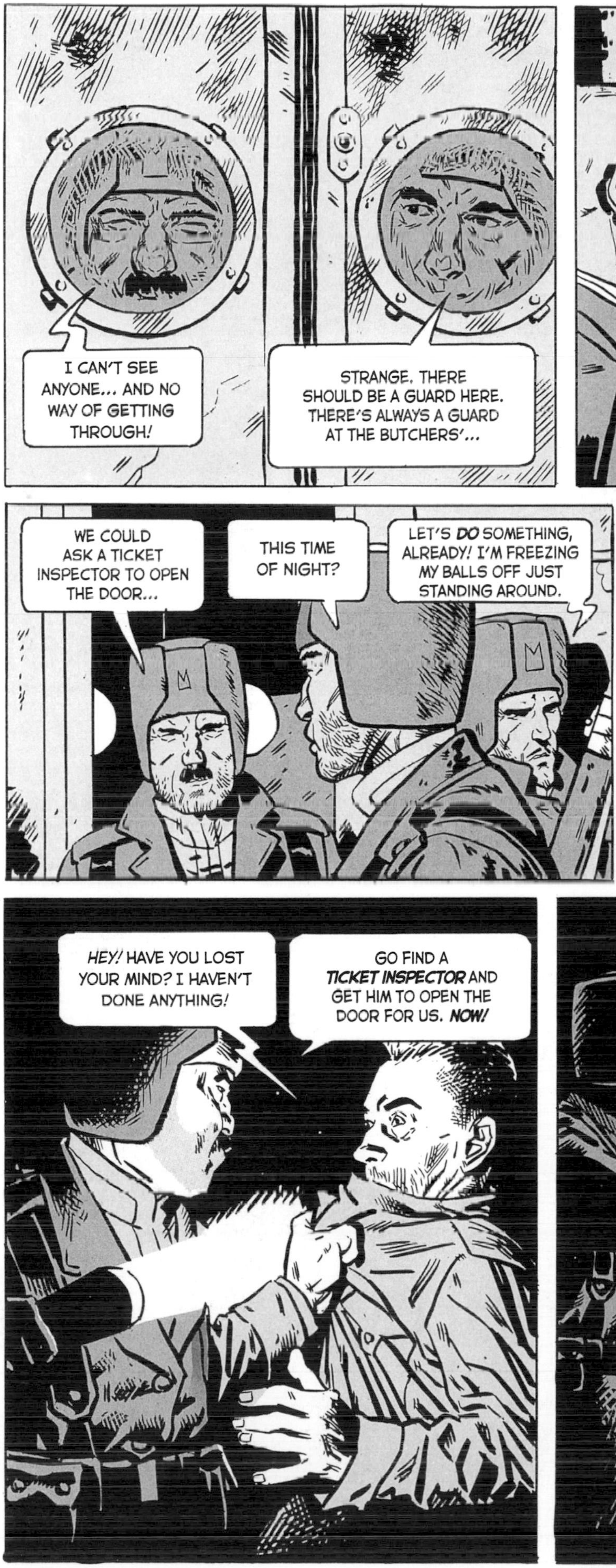
I CAN'T SEE ANYONE... AND NO WAY OF GETTING THROUGH!
STRANGE. THERE SHOULD BE A GUARD HERE. THERE'S ALWAYS A GUARD AT THE BUTCHERS'...
THE BUTCHERS'?
YEAH, WHERE MAMA IS. THAT'S WHERE THEY HARVEST THE SYNTHETIC MEAT FOR THE WHOLE TRAIN. I'VE DONE DUTY AS A NIGHT GUARD HERE. IT'S SEALED TIGHT AT NIGHT, BECAUSE OF THE AISLE-RATS...
WE COULD ASK A TICKET INSPECTOR TO OPEN THE DOOR...
THIS TIME OF NIGHT?
LET'S DO SOMETHING, ALREADY! I'M FREEZING MY BALLS OFF JUST STANDING AROUND.
WHAT'S THE PLAN?
LOCO, WILL YOU GIVE IT A REST...
HEY! HAVE YOU LOST YOUR MIND? I HAVEN'T DONE ANYTHING!
GO FIND A TICKET INSPECTOR AND GET HIM TO OPEN THE DOOR FOR US. NOW!
HOW?! I DON'T KNOW WHERE HE IS!
JUST BLOODY WELL DO IT! MOVE! OR I'LL BEAT THE SHIT OUT OF YOU WITH MY FLASHLIGHT!

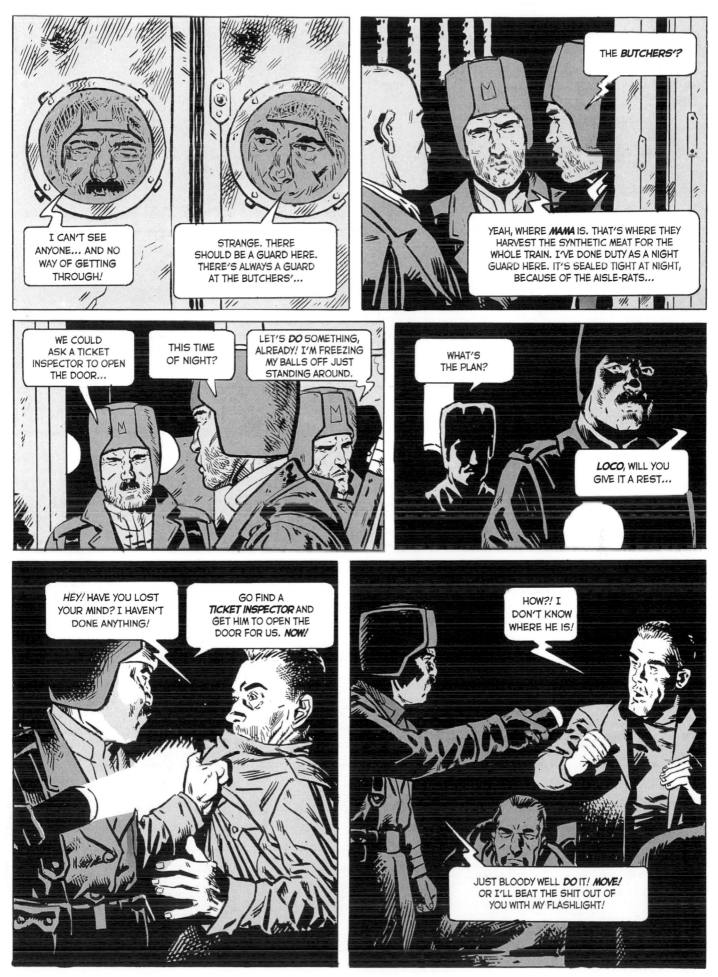

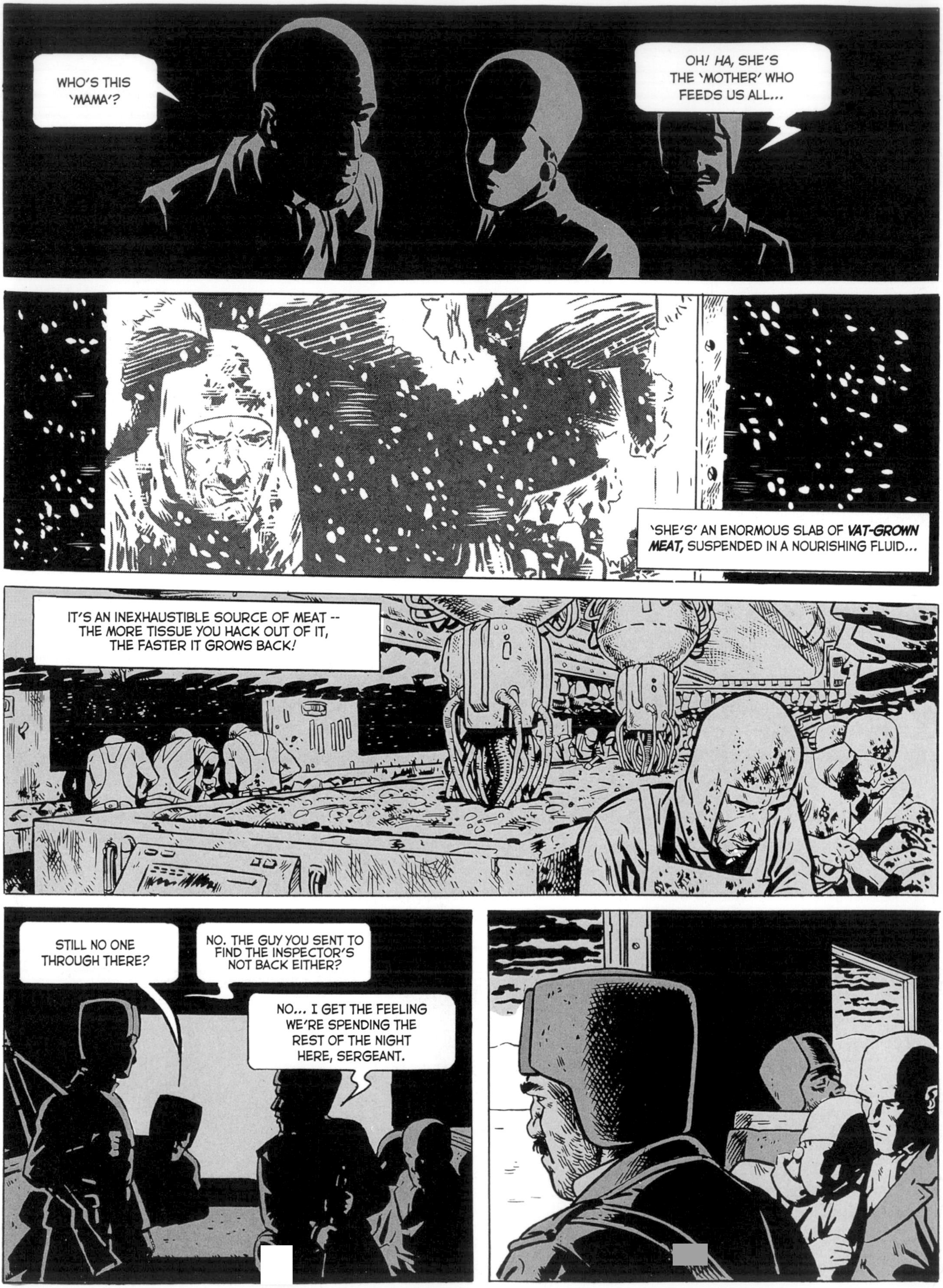
WHO'S THIS 'MAMA'?
OH! HA, SHE'S THE 'MOTHER' WHO FEEDS US ALL...
'SHE'S' AN ENORMOUS SLAB OF VAT-GROWN MEAT, SUSPENDED IN A NOURISHING FLUID...
IT'S AN INEXHAUSTIBLE SOURCE OF MEAT -- THE MORE TISSUE YOU HACK OUT OF IT, THE FASTER IT GROWS BACK!
STILL NO ONE THROUGH THERE?
NO. THE GUY YOU SENT TO FIND THE INSPECTOR'S NOT BACK EITHER?
NO... I GET THE FEELING WE'RE SPENDING THE REST OF THE NIGHT HERE, SERGEANT.

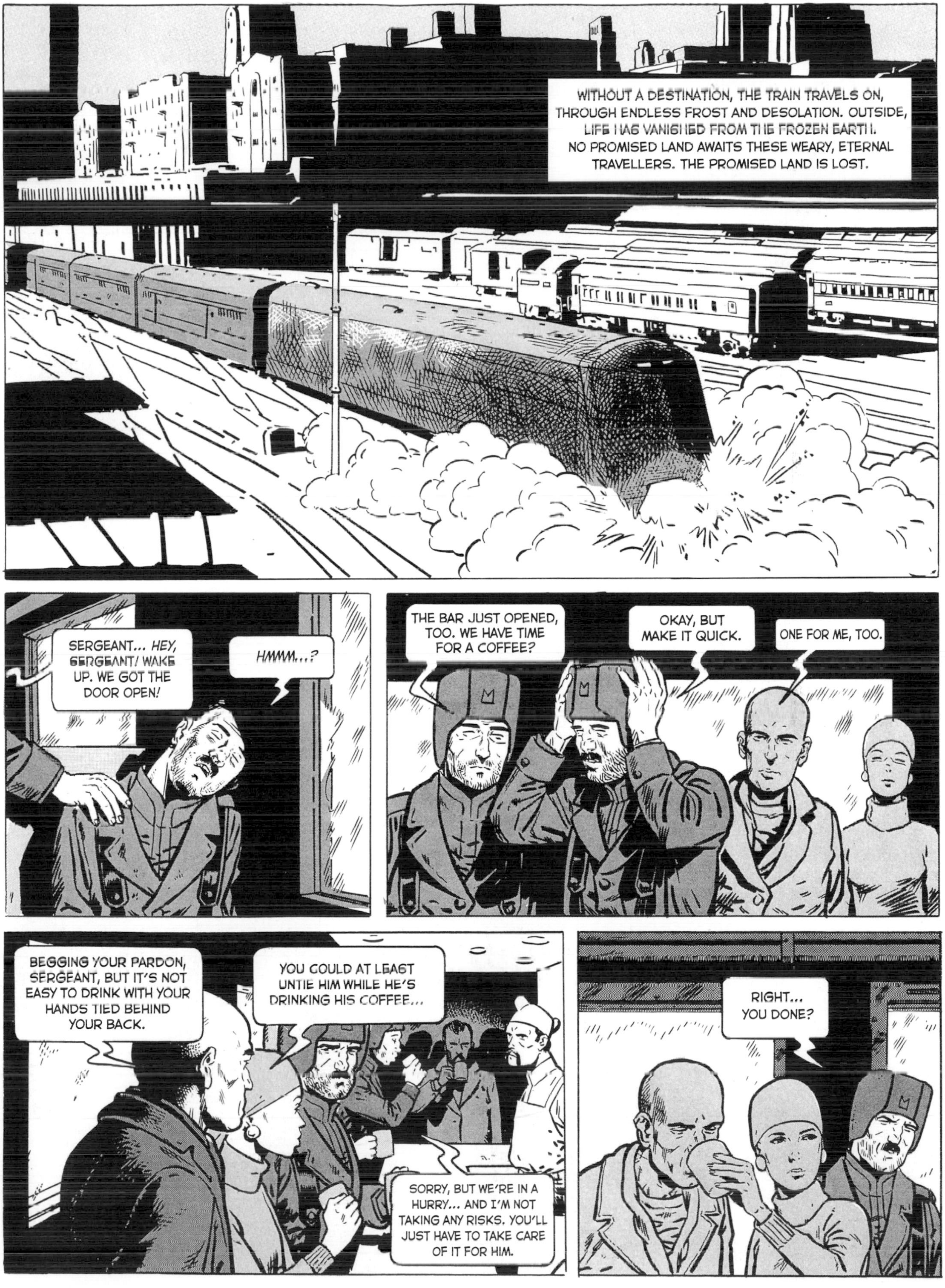
WITHOUT A DESTINATION, THE TRAIN TRAVELS ON, THROUGH ENDLESS FROST AND DESOLATION. OUTSIDE, LIFE HAS VANISHED FROM THE FROZEN EARTH. NO PROMISED LAND AWAITS THESE WEARY, ETERNAL TRAVELLERS. THE PROMISED LAND IS LOST.
SERGEANT... *HEY,* SERGEANT! WAKE UP. WE GOT THE DOOR OPEN!
HMMM...?
THE BAR JUST OPENED, TOO. WE HAVE TIME FOR A COFFEE?
OKAY, BUT MAKE IT QUICK.
ONE FOR ME, TOO.
BEGGING YOUR PARDON, SERGEANT, BUT IT'S NOT EASY TO DRINK WITH YOUR HANDS TIED BEHIND YOUR BACK.
YOU COULD AT LEAST UNTIE HIM WHILE HE'S DRINKING HIS COFFEE...
SORRY, BUT WE'RE IN A HURRY... AND I'M NOT TAKING ANY RISKS. YOU'LL JUST HAVE TO TAKE CARE OF IT FOR HIM.
RIGHT... YOU DONE?

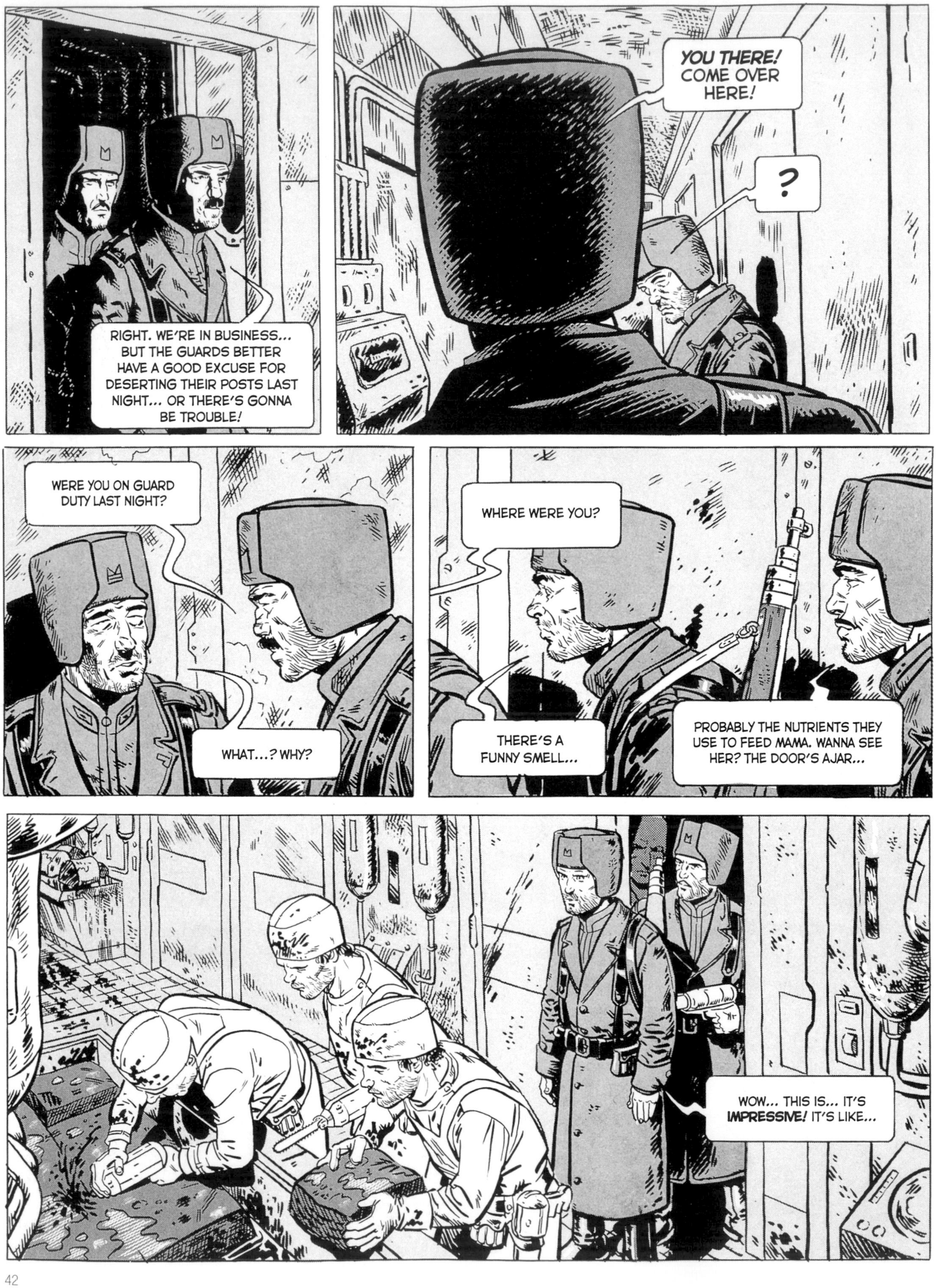
RIGHT. WE'RE IN BUSINESS... BUT THE GUARDS BETTER HAVE A GOOD EXCUSE FOR DESERTING THEIR POSTS LAST NIGHT... OR THERE'S GONNA BE TROUBLE!
YOU THERE! COME OVER HERE!
?
WERE YOU ON GUARD DUTY LAST NIGHT?
WHAT...? WHY?
WHERE WERE YOU?
THERE'S A FUNNY SMELL...
PROBABLY THE NUTRIENTS THEY USE TO FEED MAMA. WANNA SEE HER? THE DOOR'S AJAR...
WOW... THIS IS... IT'S IMPRESSIVE! IT'S LIKE...

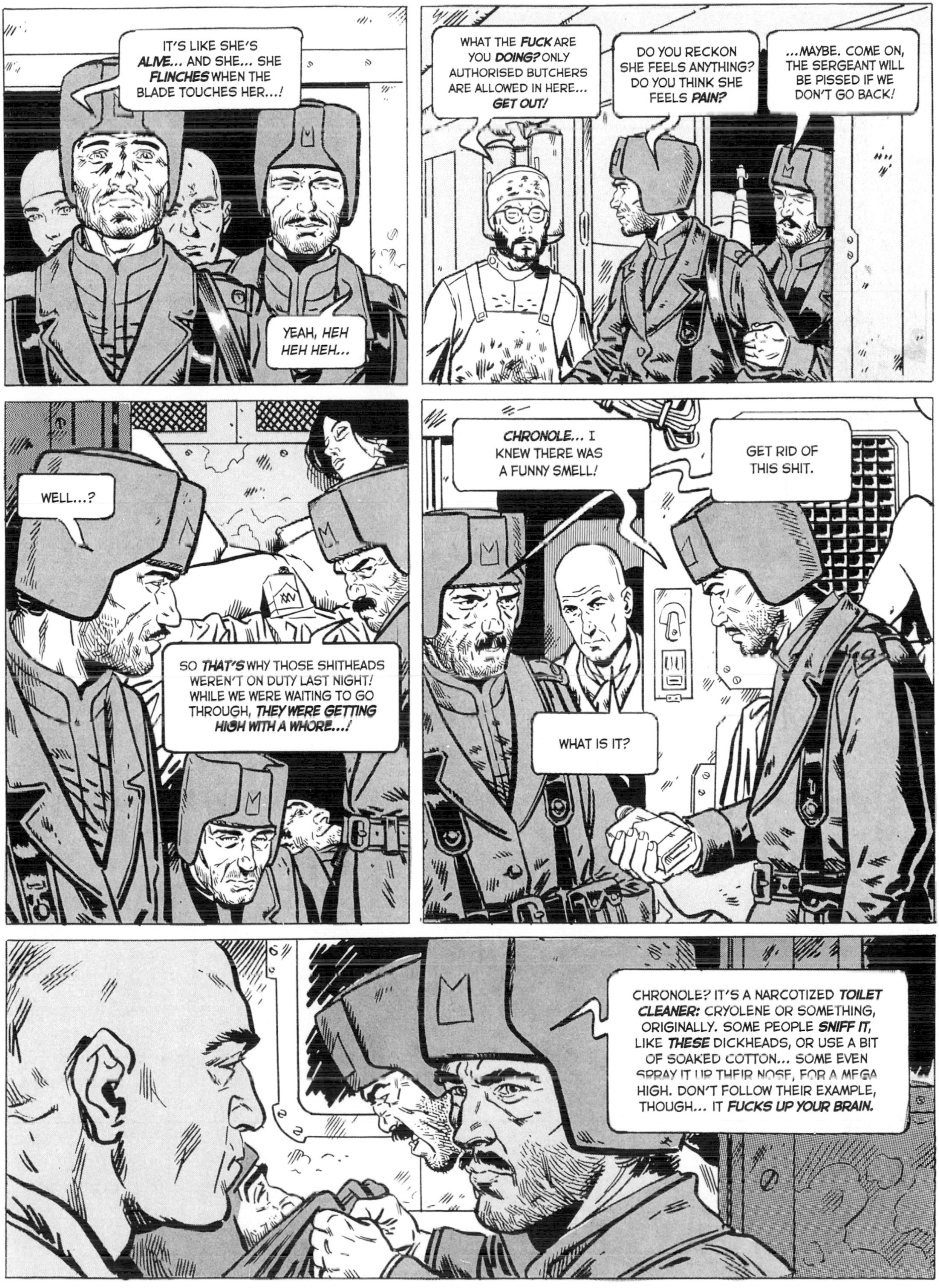
IT'S LIKE SHE'S ALIVE... AND SHE... SHE FLINCHES WHEN THE BLADE TOUCHES HER...!
YEAH, HEH HEH HEH...
WHAT THE FUCK ARE YOU DOING? ONLY AUTHORISED BUTCHERS ARE ALLOWED IN HERE... GET OUT!
DO YOU RECKON SHE FEELS ANYTHING? DO YOU THINK SHE FEELS PAIN?
...MAYBE. COME ON, THE SERGEANT WILL BE PISSED IF WE DON'T GO BACK!
WELL...?
SO THAT'S WHY THOSE SHITHEADS WEREN'T ON DUTY LAST NIGHT! WHILE WE WERE WAITING TO GO THROUGH, THEY WERE GETTING HIGH WITH A WHORE...!
CHRONOLE... I KNEW THERE WAS A FUNNY SMELL!
GET RID OF THIS SHIT.
WHAT IS IT?
CHRONOLE? IT'S A NARCOTIZED TOILET CLEANER: CRYOLENE OR SOMETHING, ORIGINALLY. SOME PEOPLE SNIFF IT, LIKE THESE DICKHEADS, OR USE A BIT OF SOAKED COTTON... SOME EVEN SPRAY IT UP THEIR NOSE, FOR A MEGA HIGH. DON'T FOLLOW THEIR EXAMPLE, THOUGH... IT FUCKS UP YOUR BRAIN.

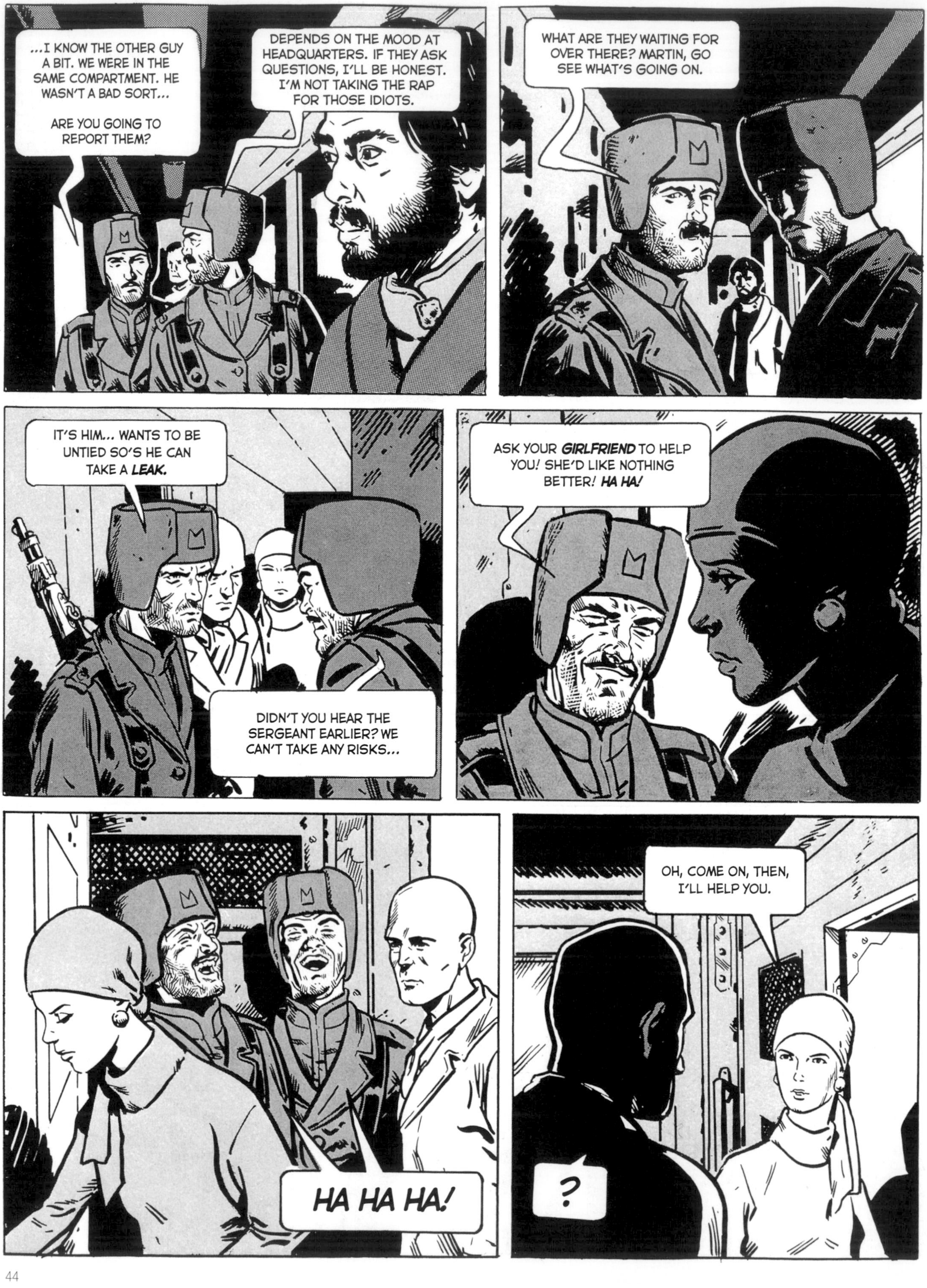
...I KNOW THE OTHER GUY A BIT. WE WERE IN THE SAME COMPARTMENT. HE WASN'T A BAD SORT...
ARE YOU GOING TO REPORT THEM?
DEPENDS ON THE MOOD AT HEADQUARTERS. IF THEY ASK QUESTIONS, I'LL BE HONEST. I'M NOT TAKING THE RAP FOR THOSE IDIOTS.
WHAT ARE THEY WAITING FOR OVER THERE? MARTIN, GO SEE WHAT'S GOING ON.
IT'S HIM... WANTS TO BE UNTIED SO'S HE CAN TAKE A ***LEAK.***
DIDN'T YOU HEAR THE SERGEANT EARLIER? WE CAN'T TAKE ANY RISKS...
ASK YOUR ***GIRLFRIEND*** TO HELP YOU! SHE'D LIKE NOTHING BETTER! ***HA HA!***
HA HA HA!
OH, COME ON, THEN, I'LL HELP YOU.
?

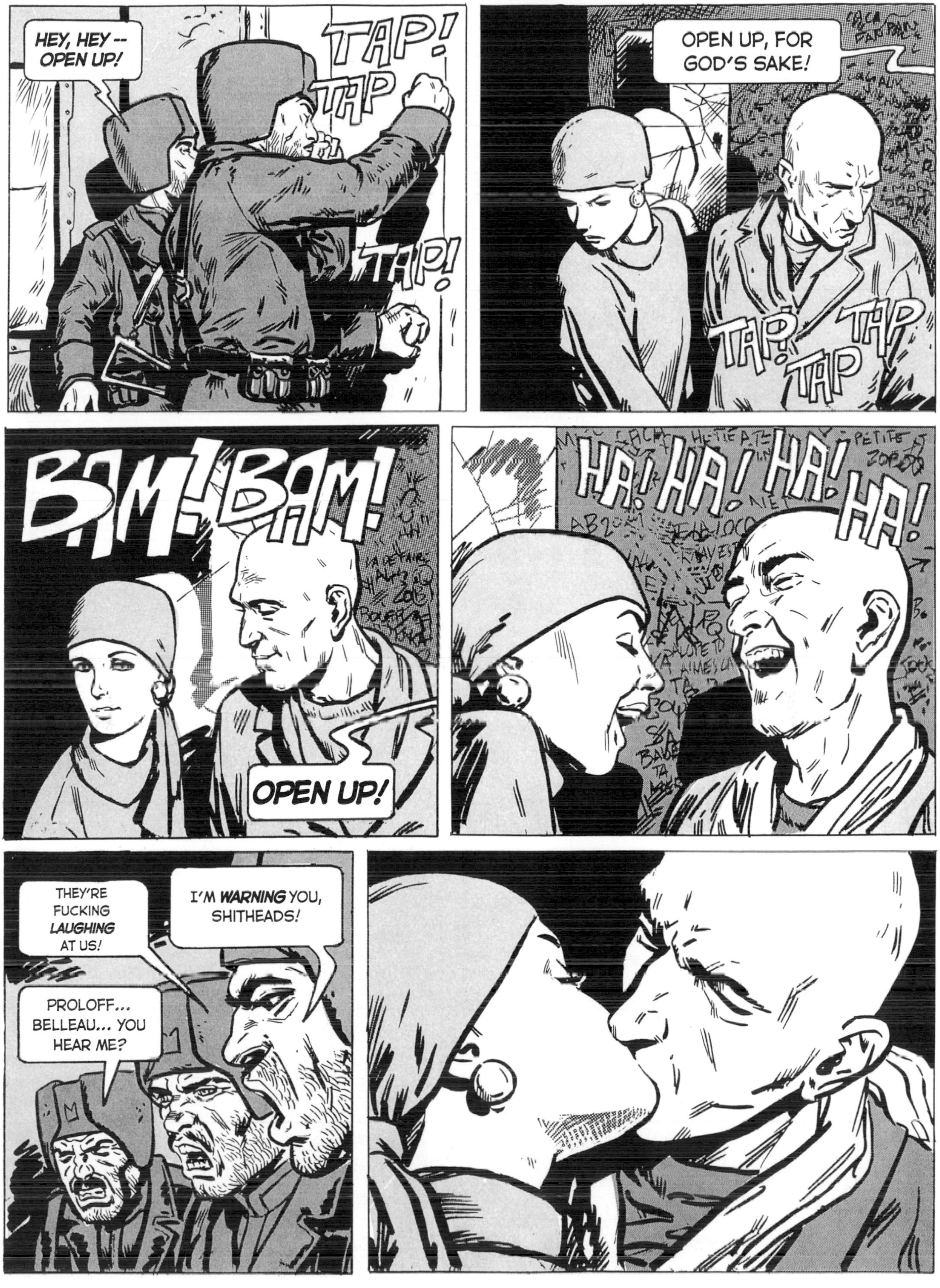

HEY, HEY -- OPEN UP!
TAP! TAP
TAP!
OPEN UP, FOR GOD'S SAKE!
TAP! TAP TAP
BAM! BAM!
OPEN UP!
HA! HA! HA! HA!
THEY'RE FUCKING LAUGHING AT US!
I'M WARNING YOU, SHITHEADS!
PROLOFF... BELLEAU... YOU HEAR ME?

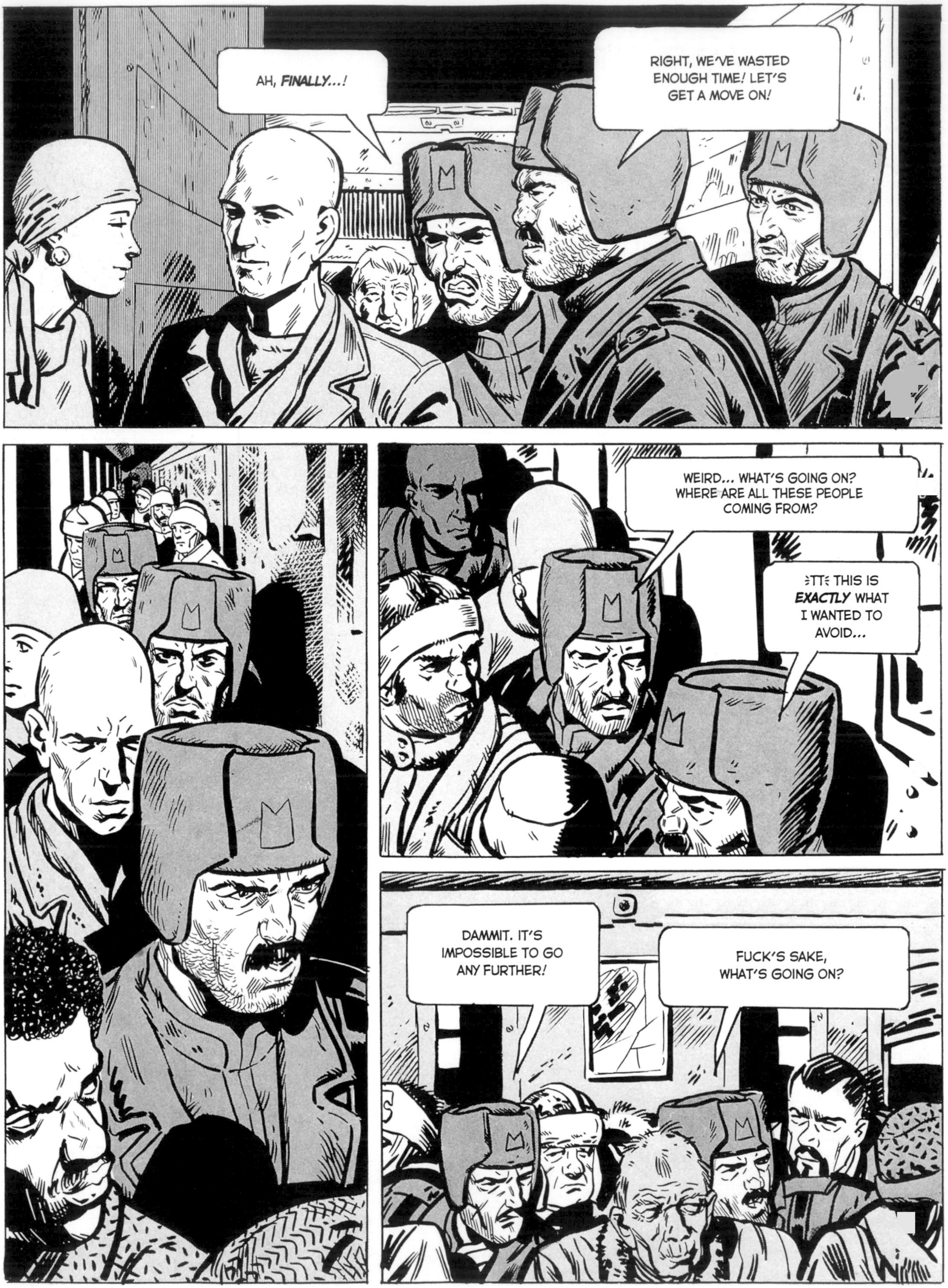
AH, **FINALLY...!**
RIGHT, WE'VE WASTED ENOUGH TIME! LET'S GET A MOVE ON!
WEIRD... WHAT'S GOING ON? WHERE ARE ALL THESE PEOPLE COMING FROM?
TT THIS IS **EXACTLY** WHAT I WANTED TO AVOID...
DAMMIT. IT'S IMPOSSIBLE TO GO ANY FURTHER!
FUCK'S SAKE, WHAT'S GOING ON?

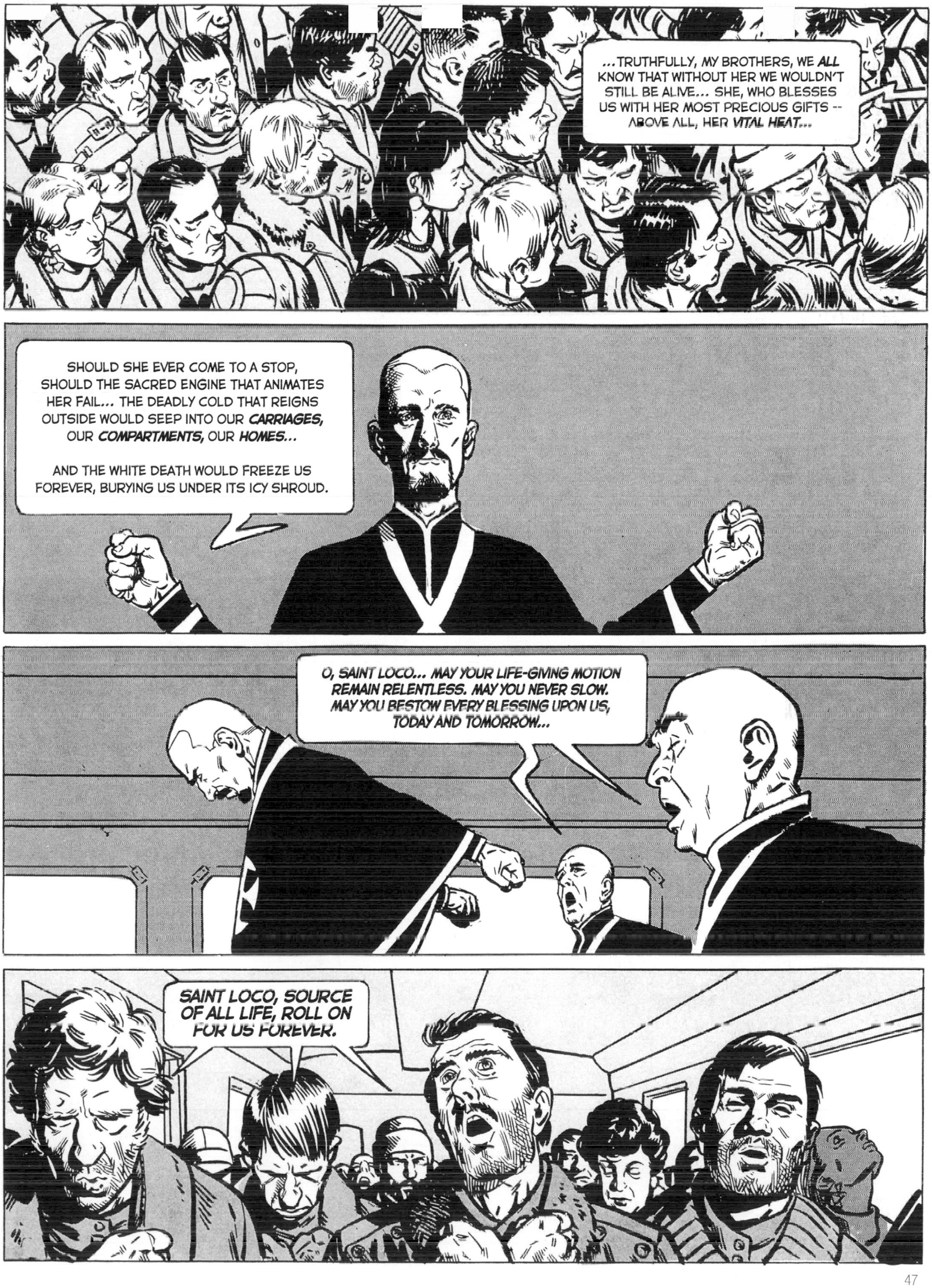
...TRUTHFULLY, MY BROTHERS, WE ALL KNOW THAT WITHOUT HER WE WOULDN'T STILL BE ALIVE... SHE, WHO BLESSES US WITH HER MOST PRECIOUS GIFTS -- ABOVE ALL, HER VITAL HEAT...
SHOULD SHE EVER COME TO A STOP, SHOULD THE SACRED ENGINE THAT ANIMATES HER FAIL... THE DEADLY COLD THAT REIGNS OUTSIDE WOULD SEEP INTO OUR CARRIAGES, OUR COMPARTMENTS, OUR HOMES...
AND THE WHITE DEATH WOULD FREEZE US FOREVER, BURYING US UNDER ITS ICY SHROUD.
O, SAINT LOCO... MAY YOUR LIFE-GIVING MOTION REMAIN RELENTLESS. MAY YOU NEVER SLOW. MAY YOU BESTOW EVERY BLESSING UPON US, TODAY AND TOMORROW...
SAINT LOCO, SOURCE OF ALL LIFE, ROLL ON FOR US FOREVER.

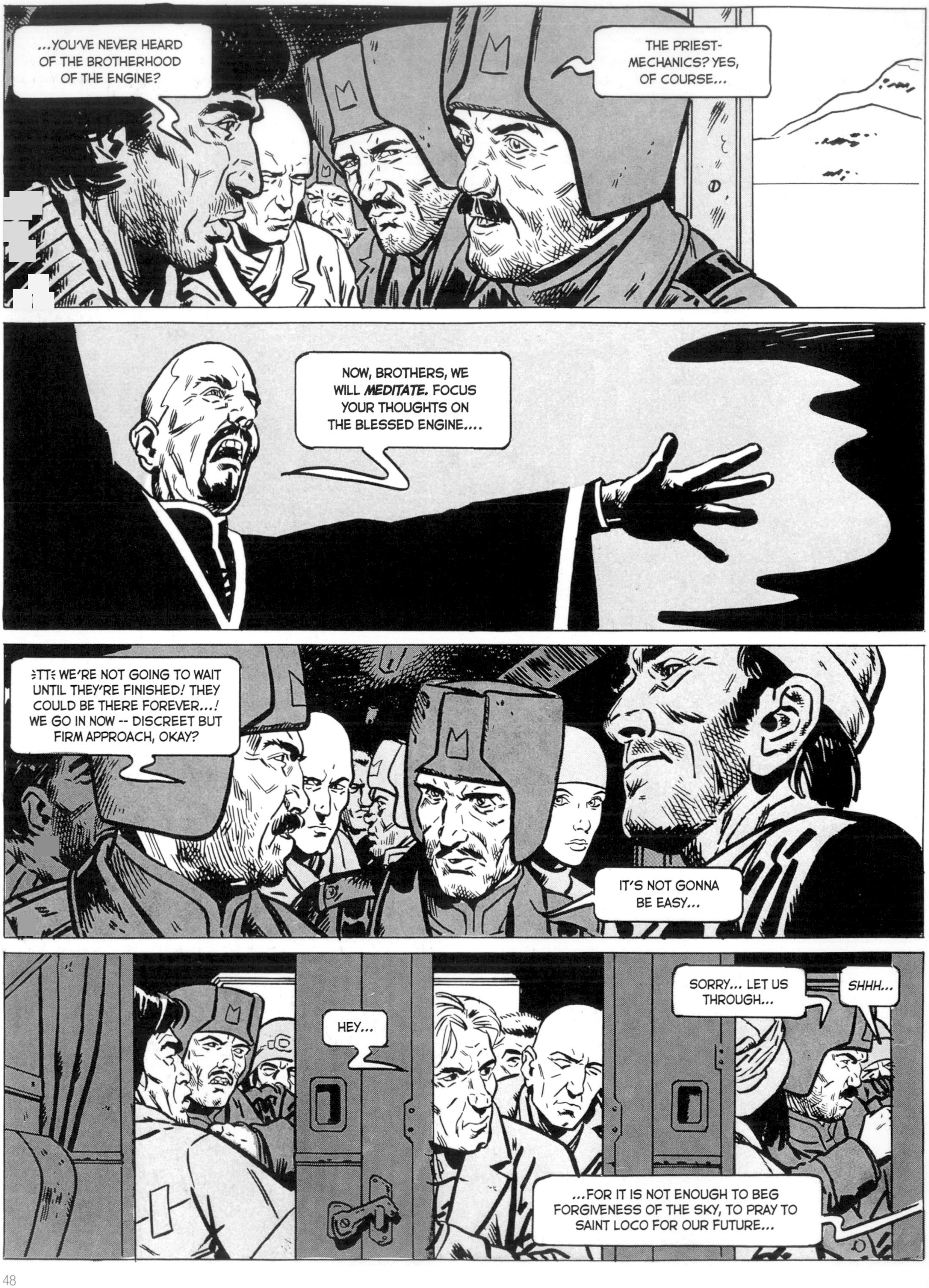
...YOU'VE NEVER HEARD OF THE BROTHERHOOD OF THE ENGINE?
THE PRIEST-MECHANICS? YES, OF COURSE...
NOW, BROTHERS, WE WILL *MEDITATE.* FOCUS YOUR THOUGHTS ON THE BLESSED ENGINE....
TT WE'RE NOT GOING TO WAIT UNTIL THEY'RE FINISHED! THEY COULD BE THERE FOREVER...! WE GO IN NOW -- DISCREET BUT FIRM APPROACH, OKAY?
IT'S NOT GONNA BE EASY...
HEY...
SORRY... LET US THROUGH...
SHHH...
...FOR IT IS NOT ENOUGH TO BEG FORGIVENESS OF THE SKY, TO PRAY TO SAINT LOCO FOR OUR FUTURE...

49

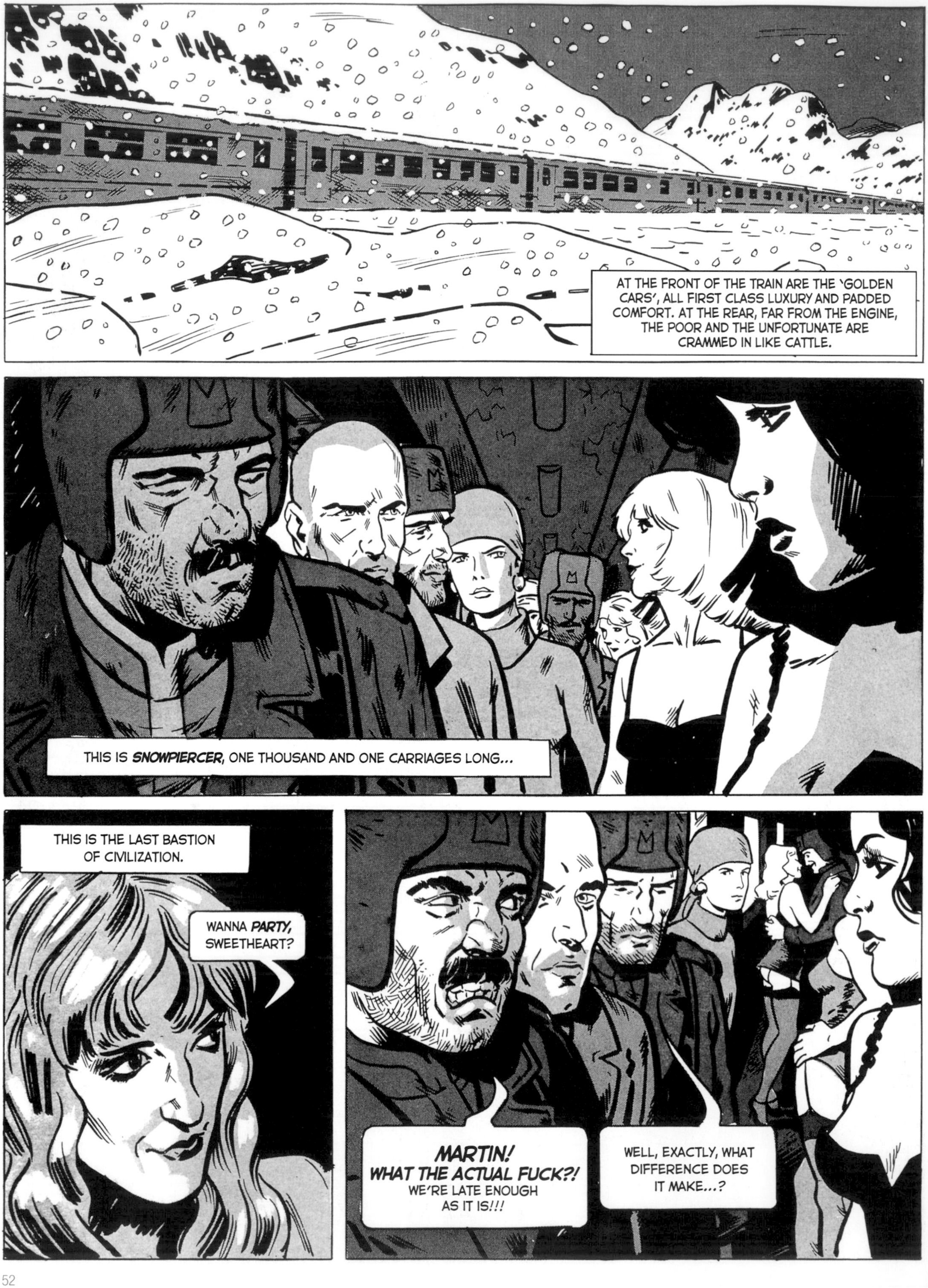
AT THE FRONT OF THE TRAIN ARE THE 'GOLDEN CARS', ALL FIRST CLASS LUXURY AND PADDED COMFORT. AT THE REAR, FAR FROM THE ENGINE, THE POOR AND THE UNFORTUNATE ARE CRAMMED IN LIKE CATTLE.
THIS IS SNOWPIERCER, ONE THOUSAND AND ONE CARRIAGES LONG...
THIS IS THE LAST BASTION OF CIVILIZATION.
WANNA PARTY, SWEETHEART?
MARTIN! WHAT THE ACTUAL FUCK?! WE'RE LATE ENOUGH AS IT IS!!!
WELL, EXACTLY, WHAT DIFFERENCE DOES IT MAKE...?

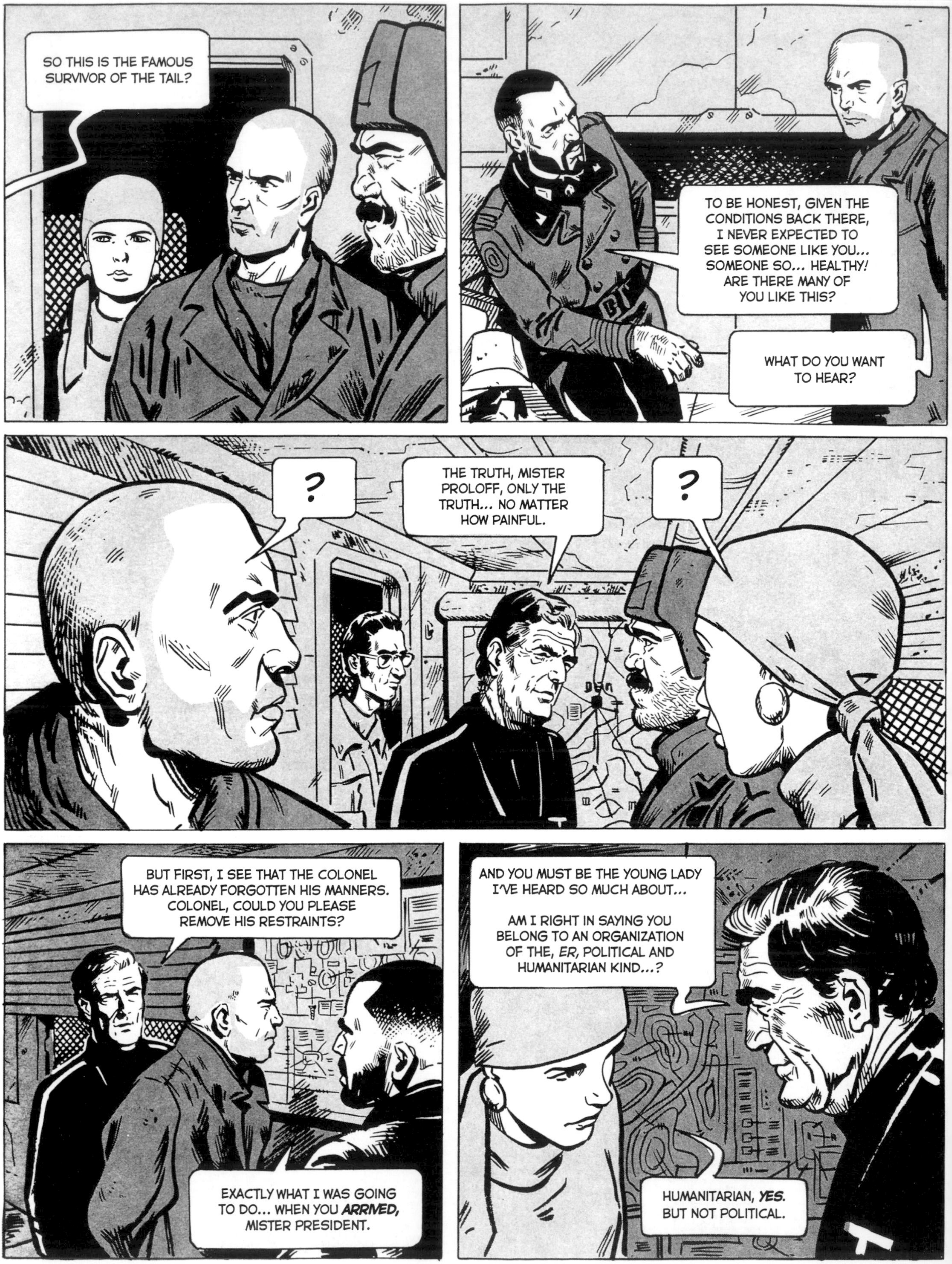
SO THIS IS THE FAMOUS SURVIVOR OF THE TAIL?
TO BE HONEST, GIVEN THE CONDITIONS BACK THERE, I NEVER EXPECTED TO SEE SOMEONE LIKE YOU... SOMEONE SO... HEALTHY! ARE THERE MANY OF YOU LIKE THIS?
WHAT DO YOU WANT TO HEAR?
?
THE TRUTH, MISTER PROLOFF, ONLY THE TRUTH... NO MATTER HOW PAINFUL.
?
BUT FIRST, I SEE THAT THE COLONEL HAS ALREADY FORGOTTEN HIS MANNERS. COLONEL, COULD YOU PLEASE REMOVE HIS RESTRAINTS?
EXACTLY WHAT I WAS GOING TO DO... WHEN YOU ARRIVED, MISTER PRESIDENT.
AND YOU MUST BE THE YOUNG LADY I'VE HEARD SO MUCH ABOUT...
AM I RIGHT IN SAYING YOU BELONG TO AN ORGANIZATION OF THE, ER, POLITICAL AND HUMANITARIAN KIND...?
HUMANITARIAN, YES. BUT NOT POLITICAL.

RABINOFF REIGNS OVER FOUR OR FIVE CARS, HOUSING SEVERAL THOUSAND ANIMALS. EVERYTHING'S PERFECTLY ORGANIZED TO BREED AND FEED THEM.
HE BREEDS MICE FOR FOOD TOO...

WHERE DO THE RABBITS COME FROM? DID HE ORGANISE ALL OF THIS?

SNOWPIERCER WAS A PLEASURE TRAIN BEFORE THE CATASTROPHE, REMEMBER? A TRAIN DESIGNED TO BE FULLY SELF-SUFFICIENT, WITHOUT SCHEDULED STOPS OR RESUPPLY, FOR WEEKS AT A TIME...!

THAT'S PROBABLY WHAT SAVED OUR LIVES...

YOURS, CERTAINLY!

YOU'RE RIGHT, I'M SORRY. I KEEP FORGETTING ALL THE OTHER, *ER...* UNDERPRIVILEGED SOULS, LIKE YOU...

IN ANY CASE, THE RABBITS ARE WELL GUARDED.

AND ALL BECAUSE OF THE FEMALE RABBITS!

WHAT DO YOU MEAN?

THEY'RE WHAT LET RABINOFF BUILD HIS EMPIRE! HE'S GOT THE ONLY DOES ON THE WHOLE TRAIN. HE'S GOT A MONOPOLY ON REPRODUCTION -- AND RULES THE MARKET AS A RESULT. IT'S IMPOSSIBLE TO GET HOLD OF A FEMALE OTHERWISE -- SO THEY'RE WELL GUARDED...

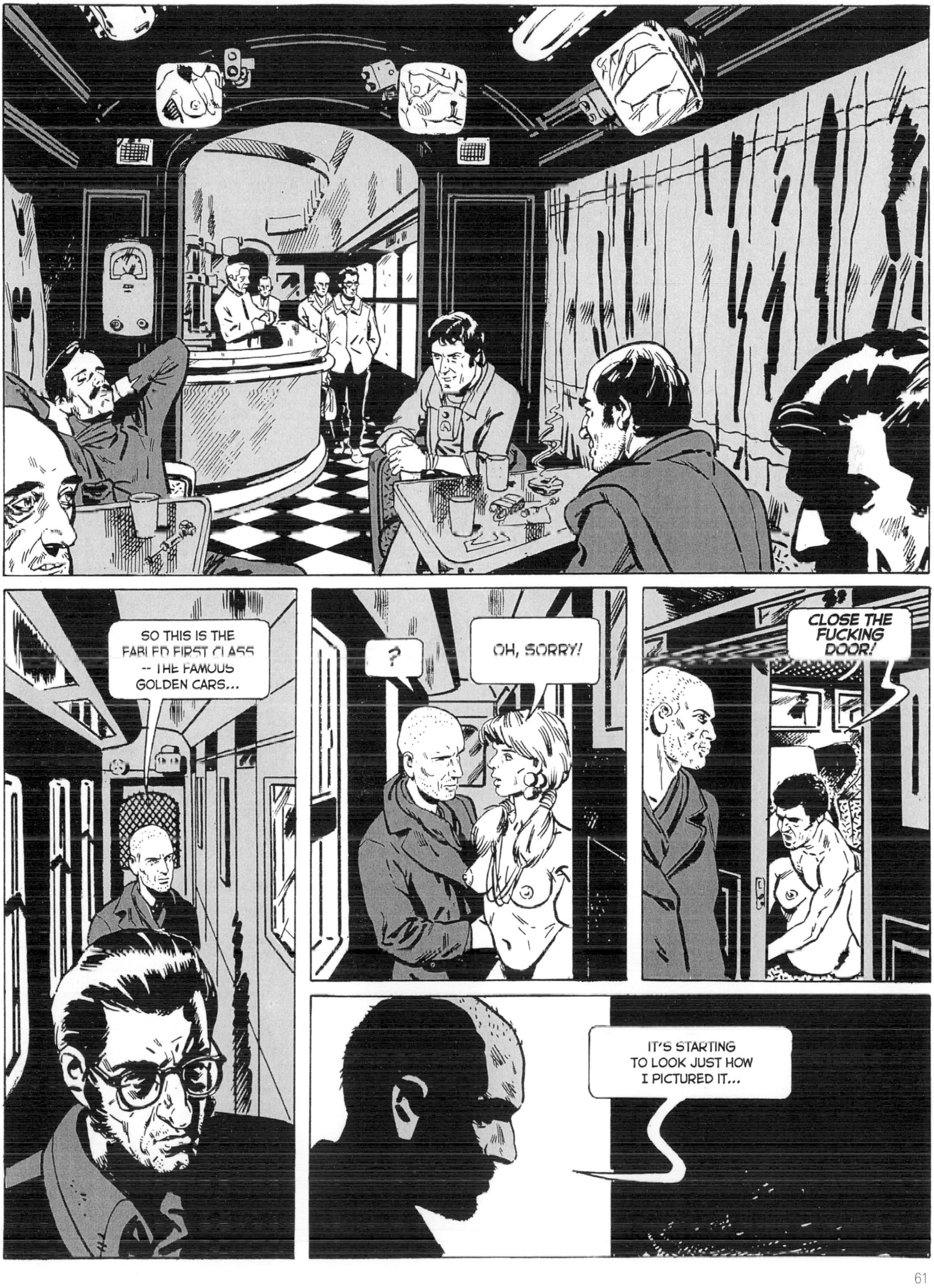
SO THIS IS THE FABLED FIRST CLASS -- THE FAMOUS GOLDEN CARS...
?
OH, SORRY!
CLOSE THE FUCKING DOOR!
IT'S STARTING TO LOOK JUST HOW I PICTURED IT...

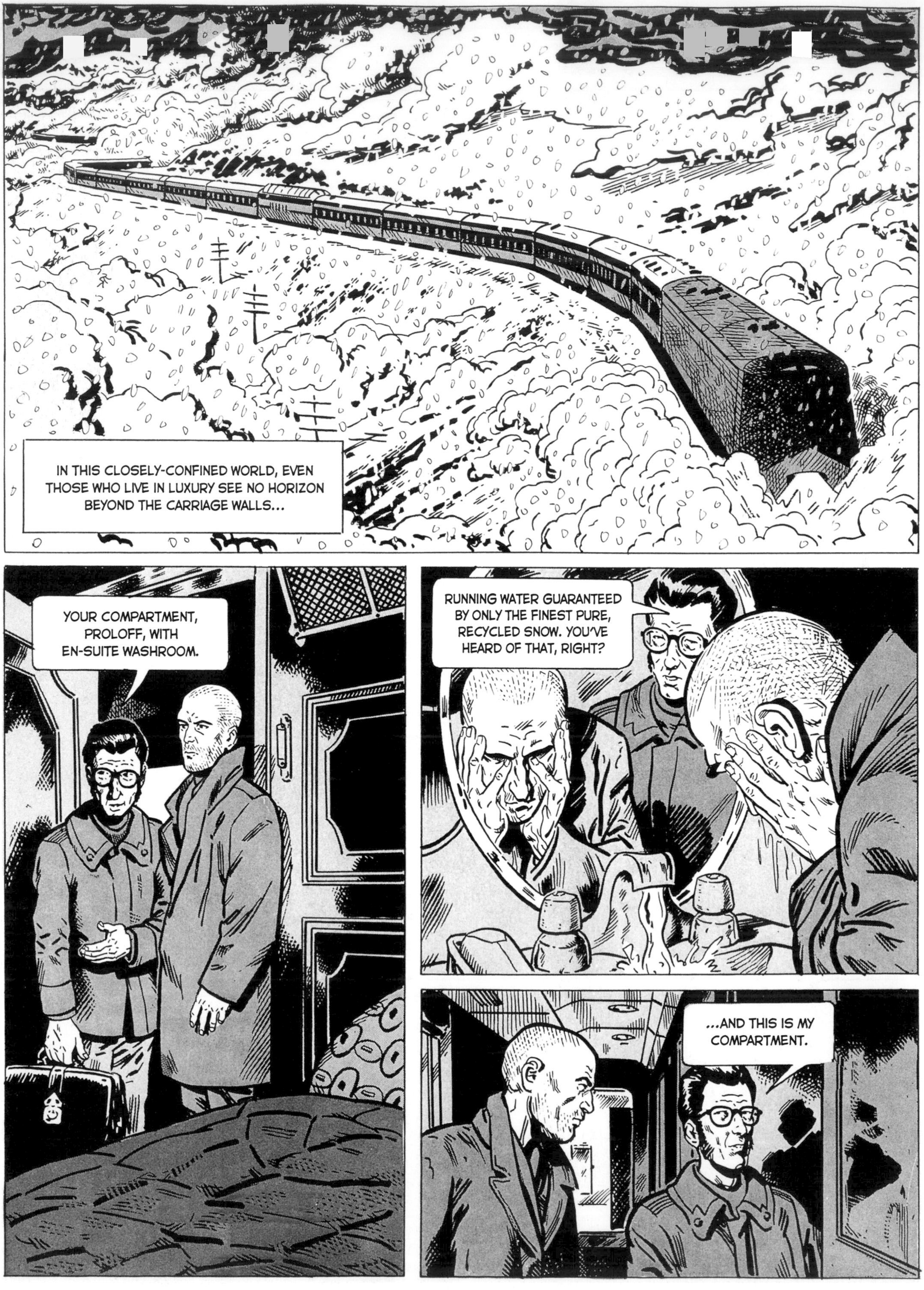

IN THIS CLOSELY-CONFINED WORLD, EVEN THOSE WHO LIVE IN LUXURY SEE NO HORIZON BEYOND THE CARRIAGE WALLS...
YOUR COMPARTMENT, PROLOFF, WITH EN-SUITE WASHROOM.
RUNNING WATER GUARANTEED BY ONLY THE FINEST PURE, RECYCLED SNOW. YOU'VE HEARD OF THAT, RIGHT?
...AND THIS IS MY COMPARTMENT.

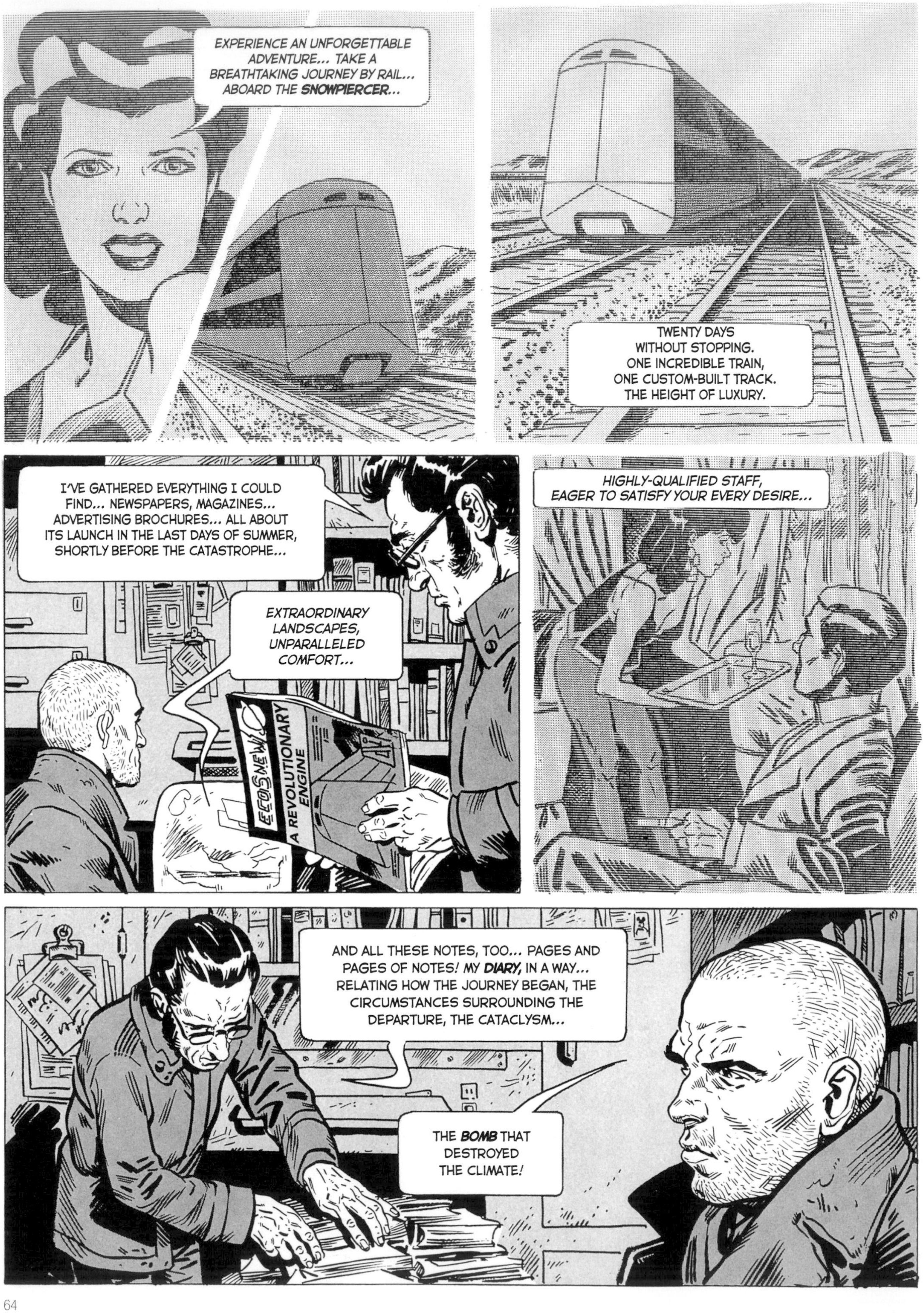

EXPERIENCE AN UNFORGETTABLE ADVENTURE... TAKE A BREATHTAKING JOURNEY BY RAIL... ABOARD THE SNOWPIERCER...
TWENTY DAYS WITHOUT STOPPING. ONE INCREDIBLE TRAIN, ONE CUSTOM-BUILT TRACK. THE HEIGHT OF LUXURY.
I'VE GATHERED EVERYTHING I COULD FIND... NEWSPAPERS, MAGAZINES... ADVERTISING BROCHURES... ALL ABOUT ITS LAUNCH IN THE LAST DAYS OF SUMMER, SHORTLY BEFORE THE CATASTROPHE...
EXTRAORDINARY LANDSCAPES, UNPARALLELED COMFORT...
ECOSNEWS
A REVOLUTIONARY ENGINE
HIGHLY-QUALIFIED STAFF, EAGER TO SATISFY YOUR EVERY DESIRE...
AND ALL THESE NOTES, TOO... PAGES AND PAGES OF NOTES! MY DIARY, IN A WAY... RELATING HOW THE JOURNEY BEGAN, THE CIRCUMSTANCES SURROUNDING THE DEPARTURE, THE CATACLYSM...
THE BOMB THAT DESTROYED THE CLIMATE!

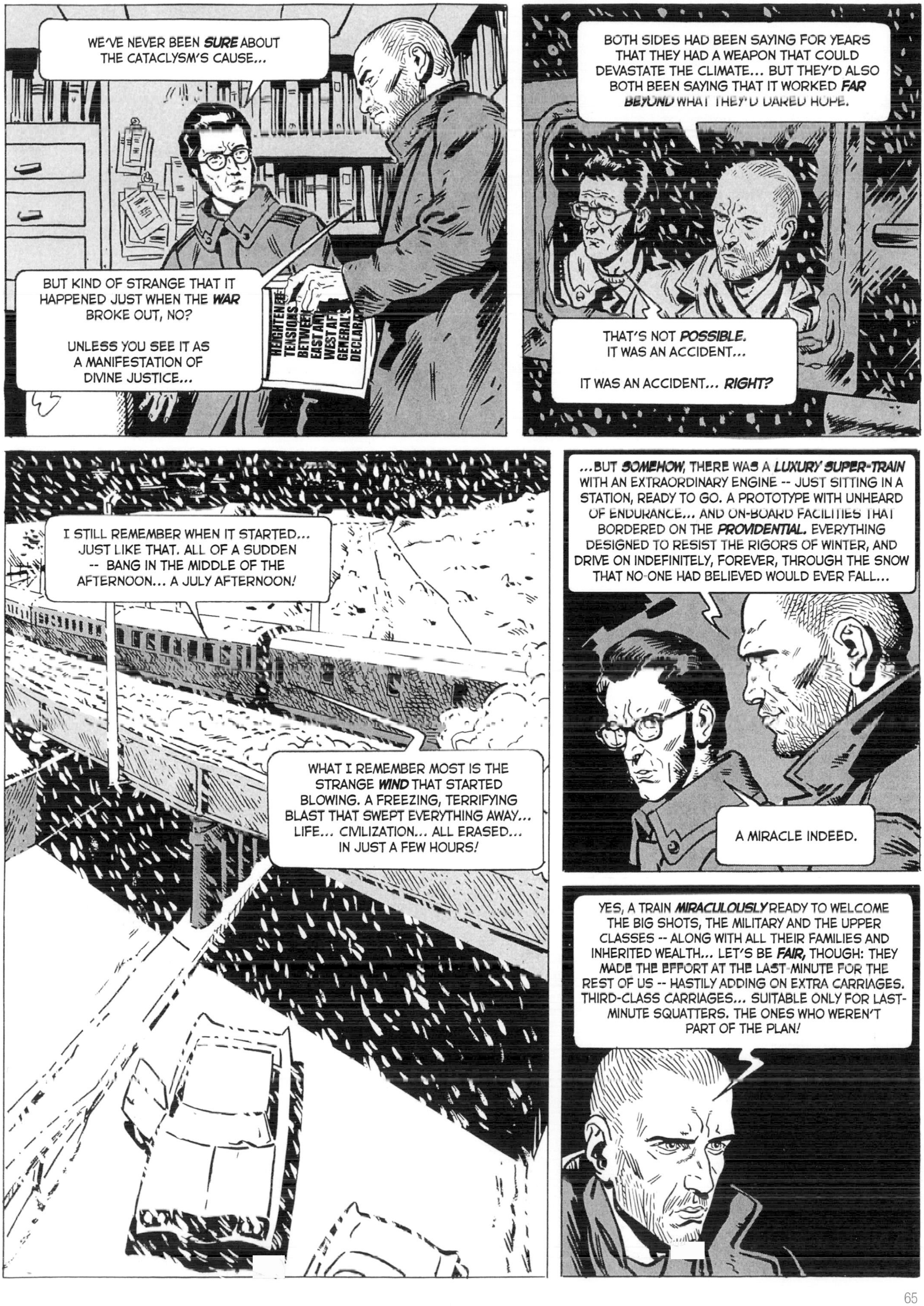

WE'VE NEVER BEEN *SURE* ABOUT THE CATACLYSM'S CAUSE...
BUT KIND OF STRANGE THAT IT HAPPENED JUST WHEN THE *WAR* BROKE OUT, NO?
UNLESS YOU SEE IT AS A MANIFESTATION OF DIVINE JUSTICE...
BOTH SIDES HAD BEEN SAYING FOR YEARS THAT THEY HAD A WEAPON THAT COULD DEVASTATE THE CLIMATE... BUT THEY'D ALSO BOTH BEEN SAYING THAT IT WORKED *FAR BEYOND* WHAT THEY'D DARED HOPE.
THAT'S NOT *POSSIBLE.* IT WAS AN ACCIDENT...
IT WAS AN ACCIDENT... *RIGHT?*
I STILL REMEMBER WHEN IT STARTED... JUST LIKE THAT. ALL OF A SUDDEN -- BANG IN THE MIDDLE OF THE AFTERNOON... A JULY AFTERNOON!
WHAT I REMEMBER MOST IS THE STRANGE *WIND* THAT STARTED BLOWING. A FREEZING, TERRIFYING BLAST THAT SWEPT EVERYTHING AWAY... LIFE... CIVILIZATION... ALL ERASED... IN JUST A FEW HOURS!
...BUT *SOMEHOW*, THERE WAS A *LUXURY SUPER-TRAIN* WITH AN EXTRAORDINARY ENGINE -- JUST SITTING IN A STATION, READY TO GO. A PROTOTYPE WITH UNHEARD OF ENDURANCE... AND ON-BOARD FACILITIES THAT BORDERED ON THE *PROVIDENTIAL.* EVERYTHING DESIGNED TO RESIST THE RIGORS OF WINTER, AND DRIVE ON INDEFINITELY, FOREVER, THROUGH THE SNOW THAT NO-ONE HAD BELIEVED WOULD EVER FALL...
A MIRACLE INDEED.
YES, A TRAIN *MIRACULOUSLY* READY TO WELCOME THE BIG SHOTS, THE MILITARY AND THE UPPER CLASSES -- ALONG WITH ALL THEIR FAMILIES AND INHERITED WEALTH... LET'S BE *FAIR,* THOUGH: THEY MADE THE EFFORT AT THE LAST-MINUTE FOR THE REST OF US -- HASTILY ADDING ON EXTRA CARRIAGES. THIRD-CLASS CARRIAGES... SUITABLE ONLY FOR LAST-MINUTE SQUATTERS. THE ONES WHO WEREN'T PART OF THE PLAN!

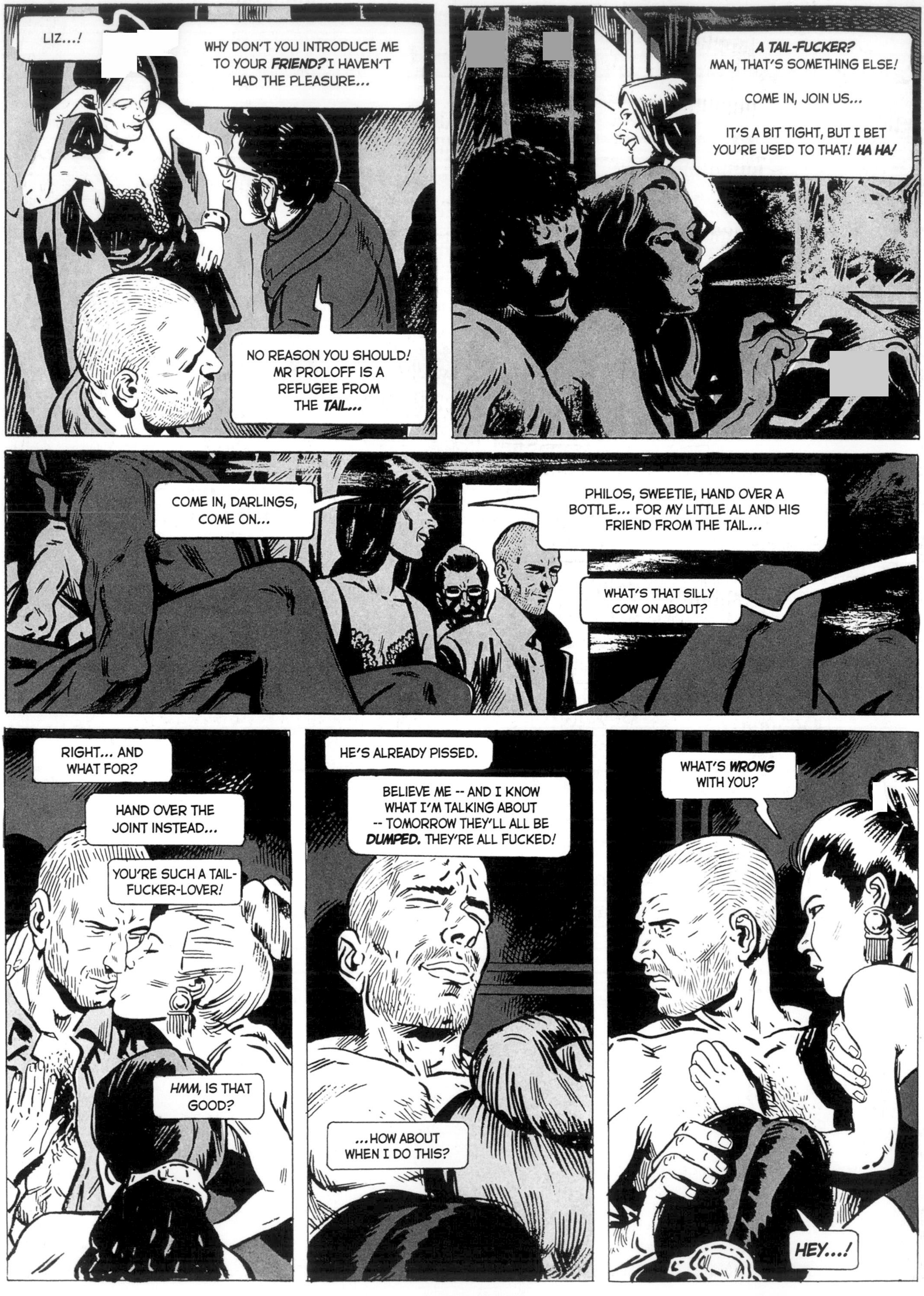
LIZ...!
WHY DON'T YOU INTRODUCE ME TO YOUR FRIEND? I HAVEN'T HAD THE PLEASURE...
NO REASON YOU SHOULD! MR PROLOFF IS A REFUGEE FROM THE TAIL...
A TAIL-FUCKER? MAN, THAT'S SOMETHING ELSE!
COME IN, JOIN US...
IT'S A BIT TIGHT, BUT I BET YOU'RE USED TO THAT! HA HA!
COME IN, DARLINGS, COME ON...
PHILOS, SWEETIE, HAND OVER A BOTTLE... FOR MY LITTLE AL AND HIS FRIEND FROM THE TAIL...
WHAT'S THAT SILLY COW ON ABOUT?
RIGHT... AND WHAT FOR?
HAND OVER THE JOINT INSTEAD...
YOU'RE SUCH A TAIL-FUCKER-LOVER!
HMM, IS THAT GOOD?
HE'S ALREADY PISSED.
BELIEVE ME -- AND I KNOW WHAT I'M TALKING ABOUT -- TOMORROW THEY'LL ALL BE DUMPED. THEY'RE ALL FUCKED!
...HOW ABOUT WHEN I DO THIS?
WHAT'S WRONG WITH YOU?
HEY...!

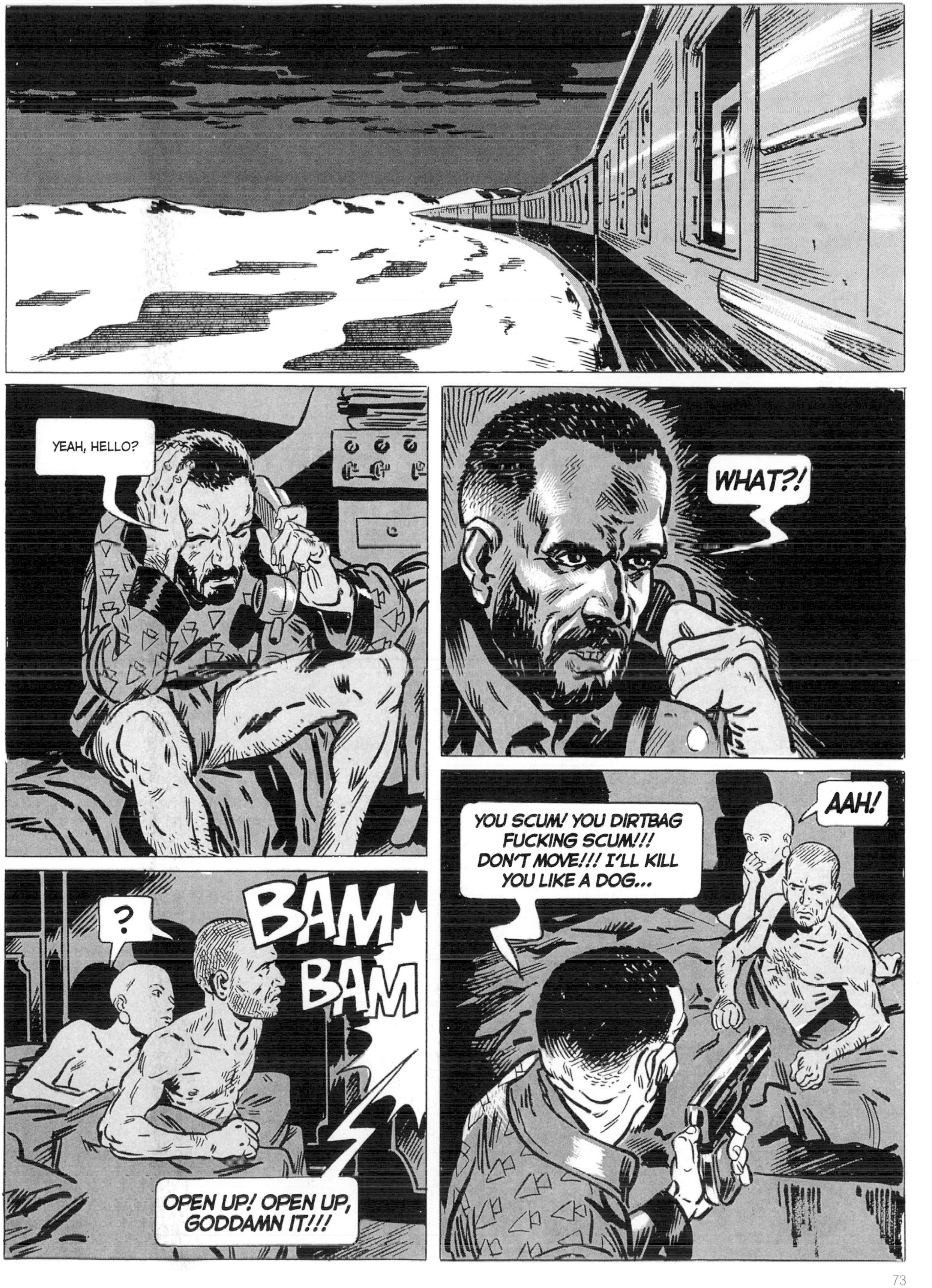
YEAH, HELLO?
WHAT?!
?
BAM BAM
OPEN UP! OPEN UP, GODDAMN IT!!!
YOU SCUM! YOU DIRTBAG FUCKING SCUM!!! DON'T MOVE!!! I'LL KILL YOU LIKE A DOG...
AAH!

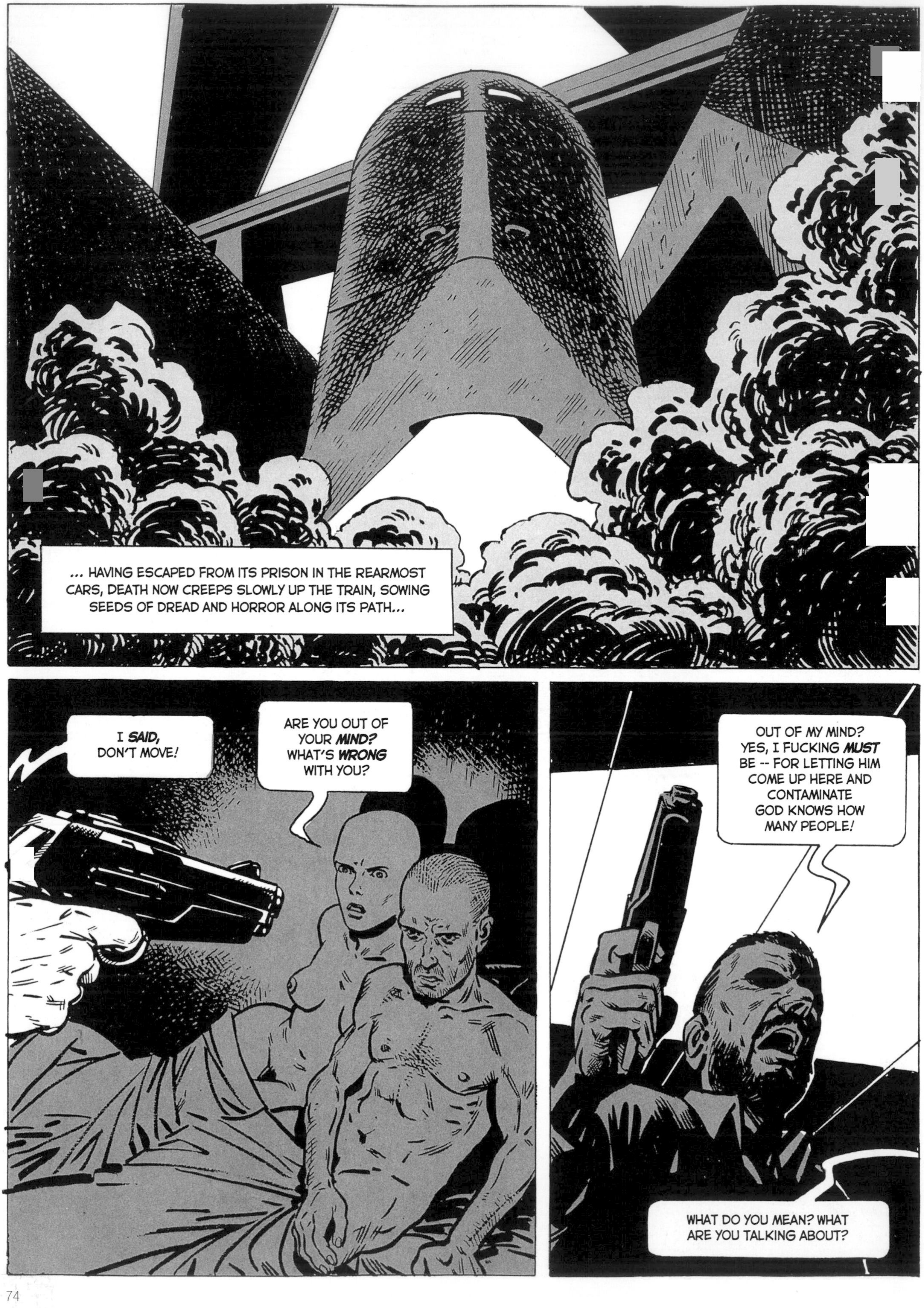
... HAVING ESCAPED FROM ITS PRISON IN THE REARMOST CARS, DEATH NOW CREEPS SLOWLY UP THE TRAIN, SOWING SEEDS OF DREAD AND HORROR ALONG ITS PATH...
I SAID, DON'T MOVE!
ARE YOU OUT OF YOUR MIND? WHAT'S WRONG WITH YOU?
OUT OF MY MIND? YES, I FUCKING MUST BE -- FOR LETTING HIM COME UP HERE AND CONTAMINATE GOD KNOWS HOW MANY PEOPLE!
WHAT DO YOU MEAN? WHAT ARE YOU TALKING ABOUT?

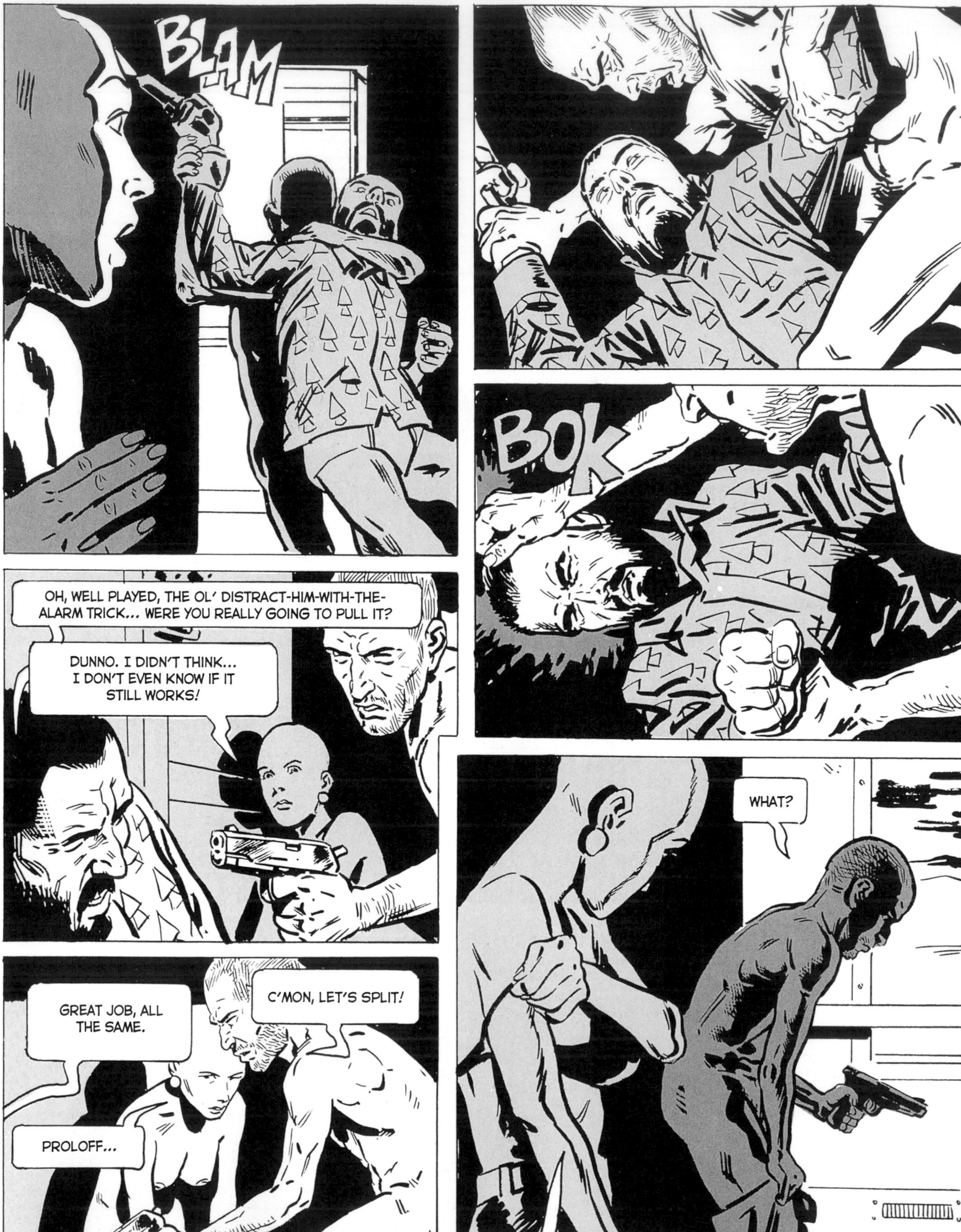
BLAM
BOK
OH, WELL PLAYED, THE OL' DISTRACT-HIM-WITH-THE-ALARM TRICK... WERE YOU REALLY GOING TO PULL IT?
DUNNO. I DIDN'T THINK... I DON'T EVEN KNOW IF IT STILL WORKS!
GREAT JOB, ALL THE SAME.
C'MON, LET'S SPLIT!
PROLOFF...
WHAT?
IS IT TRUE WHAT HE SAID...? ABOUT THE *DISEASE*...

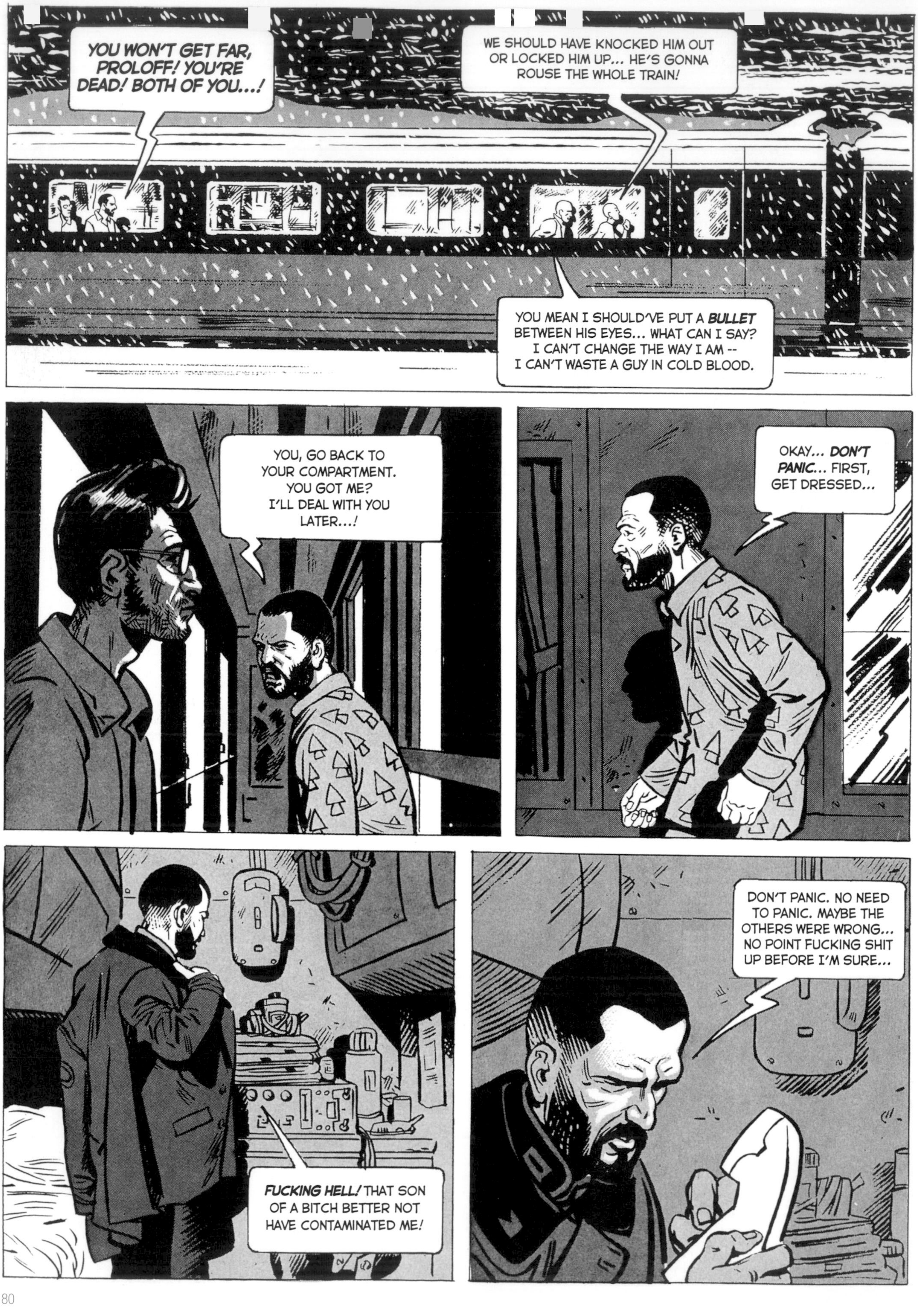
YOU WON'T GET FAR, PROLOFF! YOU'RE DEAD! BOTH OF YOU...!
WE SHOULD HAVE KNOCKED HIM OUT OR LOCKED HIM UP... HE'S GONNA ROUSE THE WHOLE TRAIN!
YOU MEAN I SHOULD'VE PUT A BULLET BETWEEN HIS EYES... WHAT CAN I SAY? I CAN'T CHANGE THE WAY I AM -- I CAN'T WASTE A GUY IN COLD BLOOD.
YOU, GO BACK TO YOUR COMPARTMENT. YOU GOT ME? I'LL DEAL WITH YOU LATER...!
OKAY... DON'T PANIC... FIRST, GET DRESSED...
FUCKING HELL! THAT SON OF A BITCH BETTER NOT HAVE CONTAMINATED ME!
DON'T PANIC. NO NEED TO PANIC. MAYBE THE OTHERS WERE WRONG... NO POINT FUCKING SHIT UP BEFORE I'M SURE...

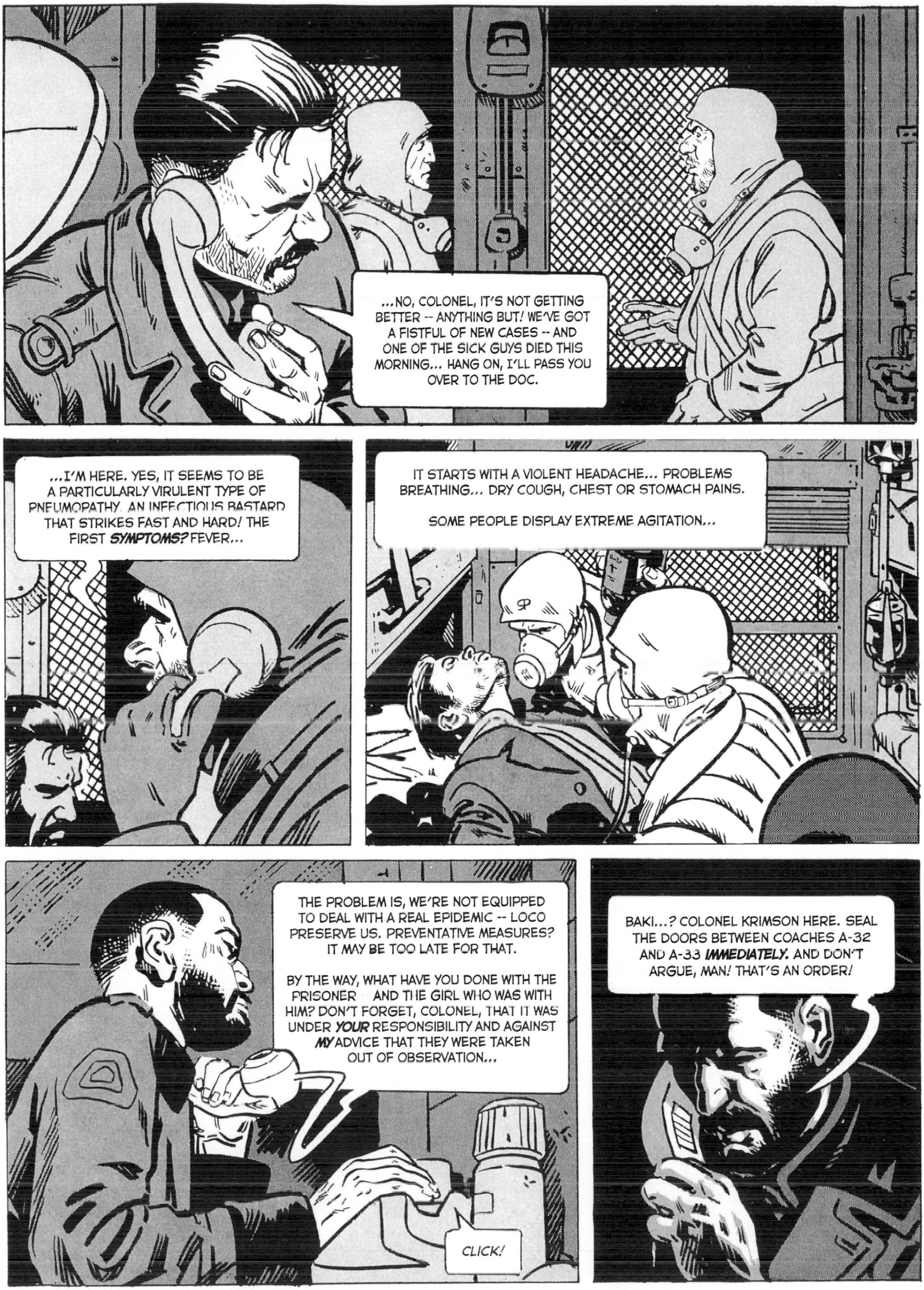
...NO, COLONEL, IT'S NOT GETTING BETTER -- ANYTHING BUT! WE'VE GOT A FISTFUL OF NEW CASES -- AND ONE OF THE SICK GUYS DIED THIS MORNING... HANG ON, I'LL PASS YOU OVER TO THE DOC.
...I'M HERE. YES, IT SEEMS TO BE A PARTICULARLY VIRULENT TYPE OF PNEUMOPATHY. AN INFECTIOUS BASTARD THAT STRIKES FAST AND HARD! THE FIRST SYMPTOMS? FEVER...
IT STARTS WITH A VIOLENT HEADACHE... PROBLEMS BREATHING... DRY COUGH, CHEST OR STOMACH PAINS.
SOME PEOPLE DISPLAY EXTREME AGITATION...
THE PROBLEM IS, WE'RE NOT EQUIPPED TO DEAL WITH A REAL EPIDEMIC -- LOCO PRESERVE US. PREVENTATIVE MEASURES? IT MAY BE TOO LATE FOR THAT.
BY THE WAY, WHAT HAVE YOU DONE WITH THE PRISONER -- AND THE GIRL WHO WAS WITH HIM? DON'T FORGET, COLONEL, THAT IT WAS UNDER YOUR RESPONSIBILITY AND AGAINST MY ADVICE THAT THEY WERE TAKEN OUT OF OBSERVATION...
CLICK!
BAKI...? COLONEL KRIMSON HERE. SEAL THE DOORS BETWEEN COACHES A-32 AND A-33 IMMEDIATELY. AND DON'T ARGUE, MAN! THAT'S AN ORDER!

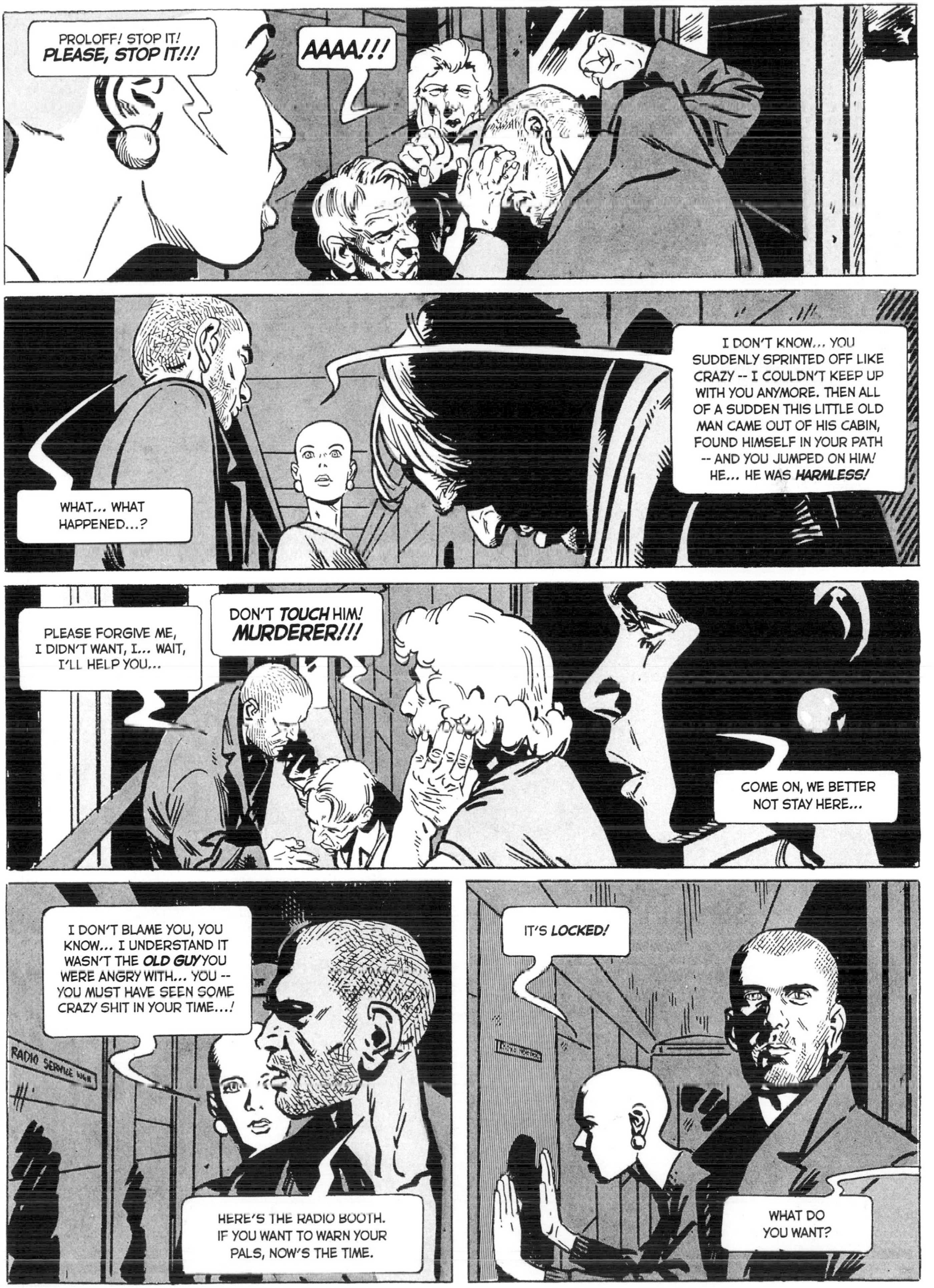

PROLOFF! STOP IT! **PLEASE, STOP IT!!!**
AAAA!!!
WHAT... WHAT HAPPENED...?
I DON'T KNOW... YOU SUDDENLY SPRINTED OFF LIKE CRAZY -- I COULDN'T KEEP UP WITH YOU ANYMORE. THEN ALL OF A SUDDEN THIS LITTLE OLD MAN CAME OUT OF HIS CABIN, FOUND HIMSELF IN YOUR PATH -- AND YOU JUMPED ON HIM! HE... HE WAS **HARMLESS!**
PLEASE FORGIVE ME, I DIDN'T WANT, I... WAIT, I'LL HELP YOU...
DON'T **TOUCH** HIM! **MURDERER!!!**
COME ON, WE BETTER NOT STAY HERE...
I DON'T BLAME YOU, YOU KNOW... I UNDERSTAND IT WASN'T THE **OLD GUY** YOU WERE ANGRY WITH... YOU -- YOU MUST HAVE SEEN SOME CRAZY SHIT IN YOUR TIME...!
HERE'S THE RADIO BOOTH. IF YOU WANT TO WARN YOUR PALS, NOW'S THE TIME.
IT'S **LOCKED!**
WHAT DO YOU WANT?

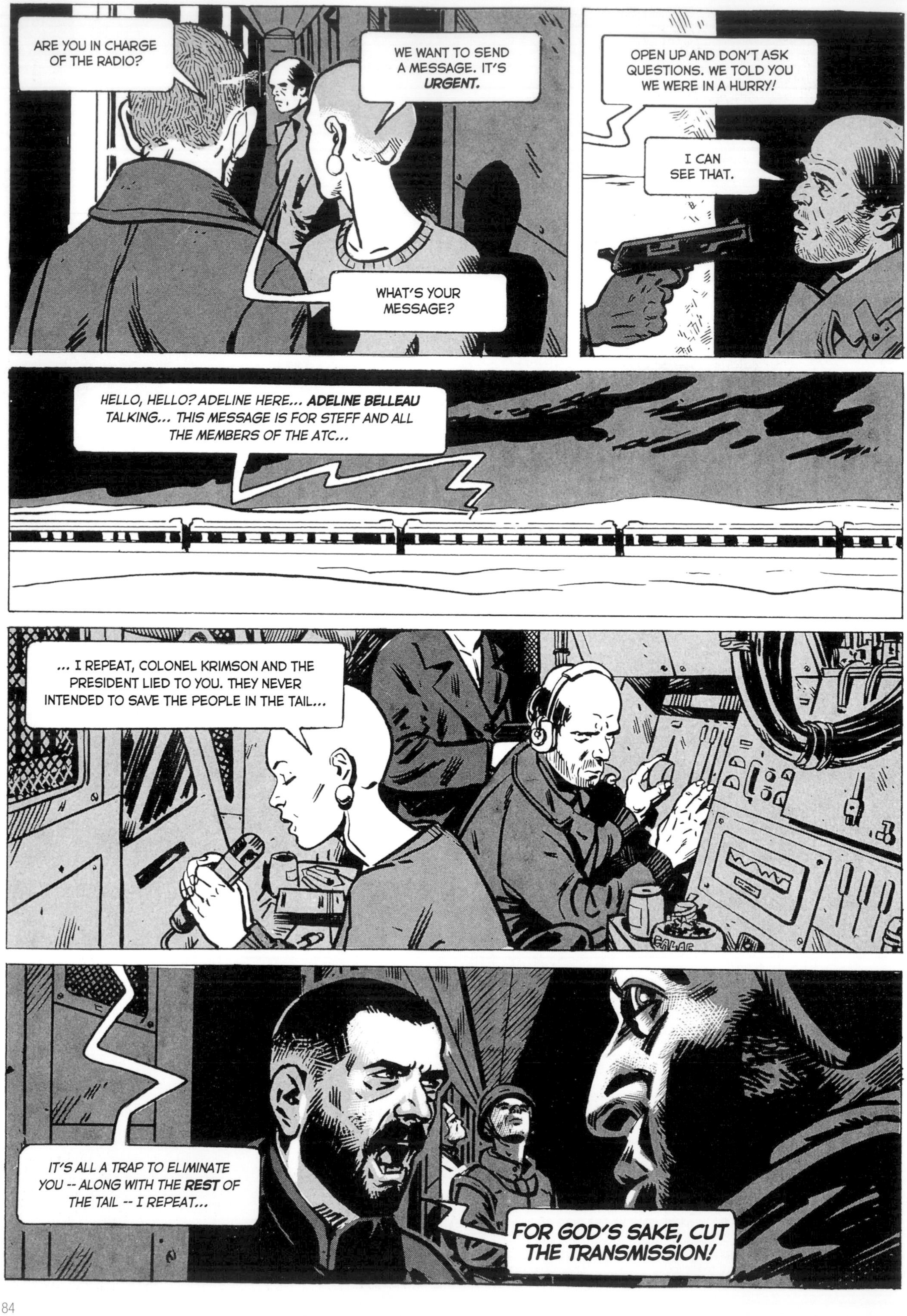
ARE YOU IN CHARGE OF THE RADIO?
WE WANT TO SEND A MESSAGE. IT'S URGENT.
WHAT'S YOUR MESSAGE?
OPEN UP AND DON'T ASK QUESTIONS. WE TOLD YOU WE WERE IN A HURRY!
I CAN SEE THAT.
HELLO, HELLO? ADELINE HERE... ADELINE BELLEAU TALKING... THIS MESSAGE IS FOR STEFF AND ALL THE MEMBERS OF THE ATC...
... I REPEAT, COLONEL KRIMSON AND THE PRESIDENT LIED TO YOU. THEY NEVER INTENDED TO SAVE THE PEOPLE IN THE TAIL...
IT'S ALL A TRAP TO ELIMINATE YOU -- ALONG WITH THE REST OF THE TAIL -- I REPEAT...
FOR GOD'S SAKE, CUT THE TRANSMISSION!

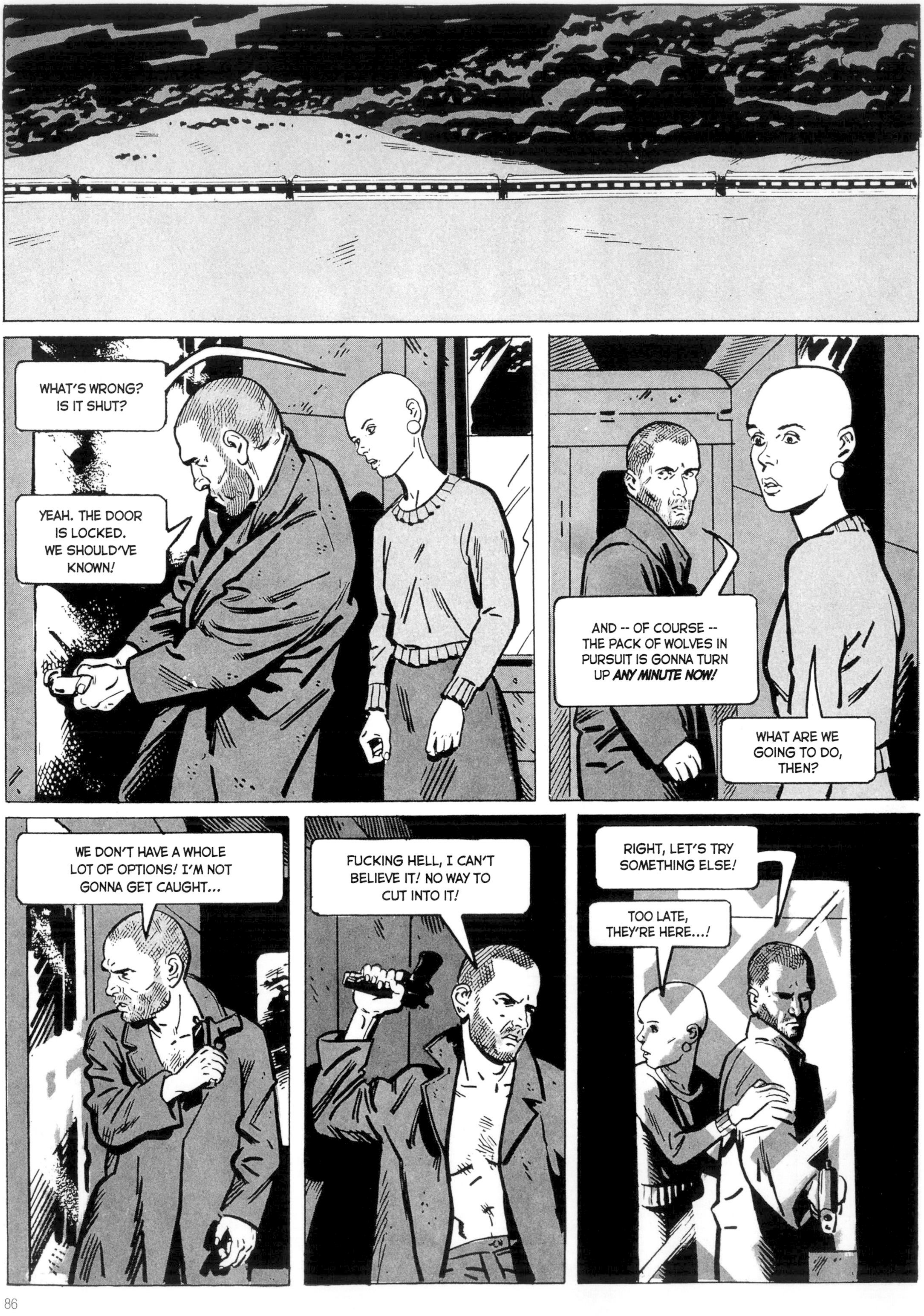
WHAT'S WRONG? IS IT SHUT?
YEAH. THE DOOR IS LOCKED. WE SHOULD'VE KNOWN!
AND -- OF COURSE -- THE PACK OF WOLVES IN PURSUIT IS GONNA TURN UP ANY MINUTE NOW!
WHAT ARE WE GOING TO DO, THEN?
WE DON'T HAVE A WHOLE LOT OF OPTIONS! I'M NOT GONNA GET CAUGHT...
FUCKING HELL, I CAN'T BELIEVE IT! NO WAY TO CUT INTO IT!
RIGHT, LET'S TRY SOMETHING ELSE!
TOO LATE, THEY'RE HERE...!

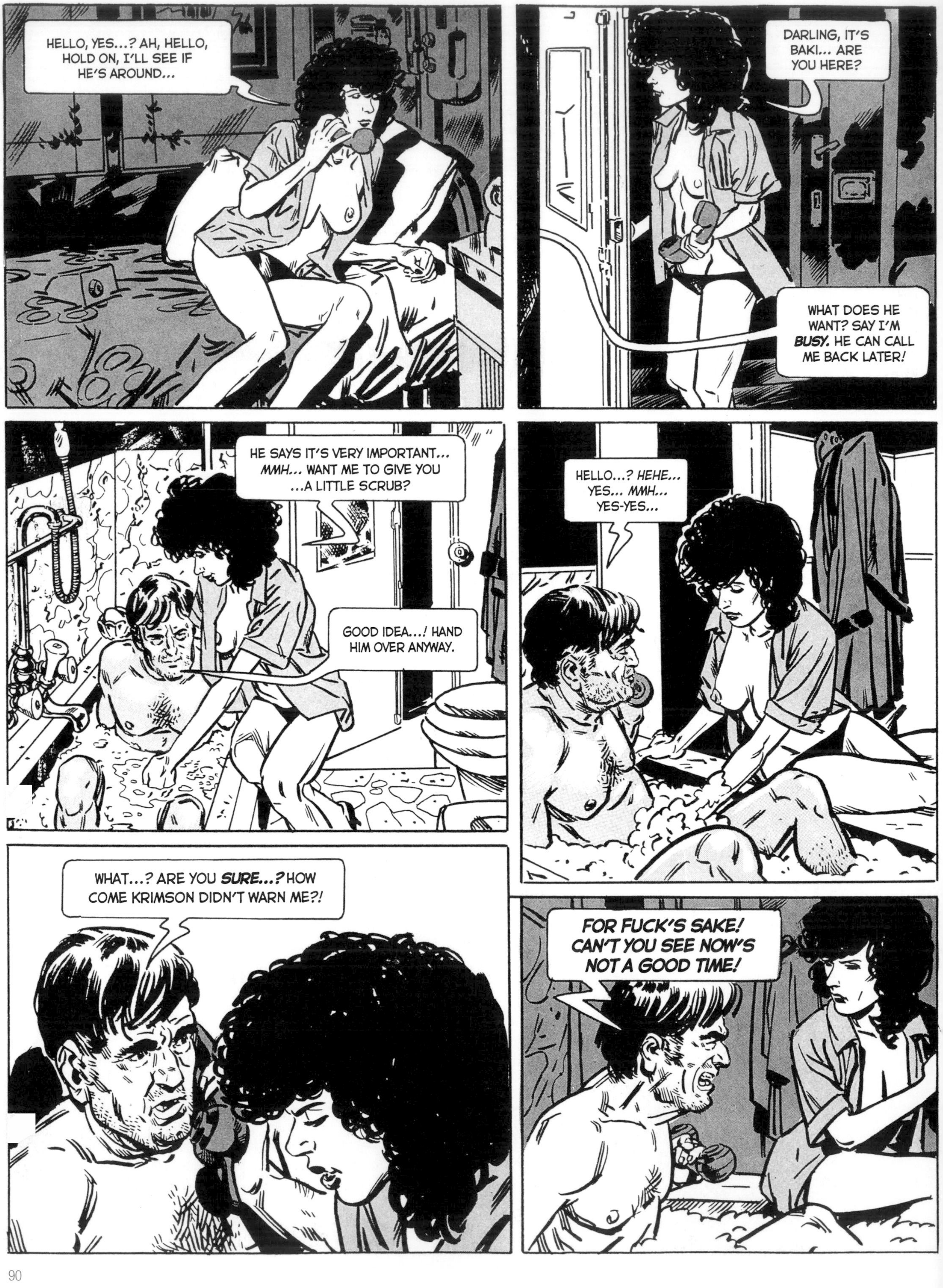
HELLO, YES...? AH, HELLO, HOLD ON, I'LL SEE IF HE'S AROUND...
DARLING, IT'S BAKI... ARE YOU HERE?
WHAT DOES HE WANT? SAY I'M **BUSY.** HE CAN CALL ME BACK LATER!
HE SAYS IT'S VERY IMPORTANT... *MMH...* WANT ME TO GIVE YOU ...A LITTLE SCRUB?
GOOD IDEA...! HAND HIM OVER ANYWAY.
HELLO...? *HEHE...* YES... *MMH...* YES-YES...
WHAT...? ARE YOU **SURE...?** HOW COME KRIMSON DIDN'T WARN ME?!
FOR FUCK'S SAKE! CAN'T YOU SEE NOW'S NOT A GOOD TIME!

91

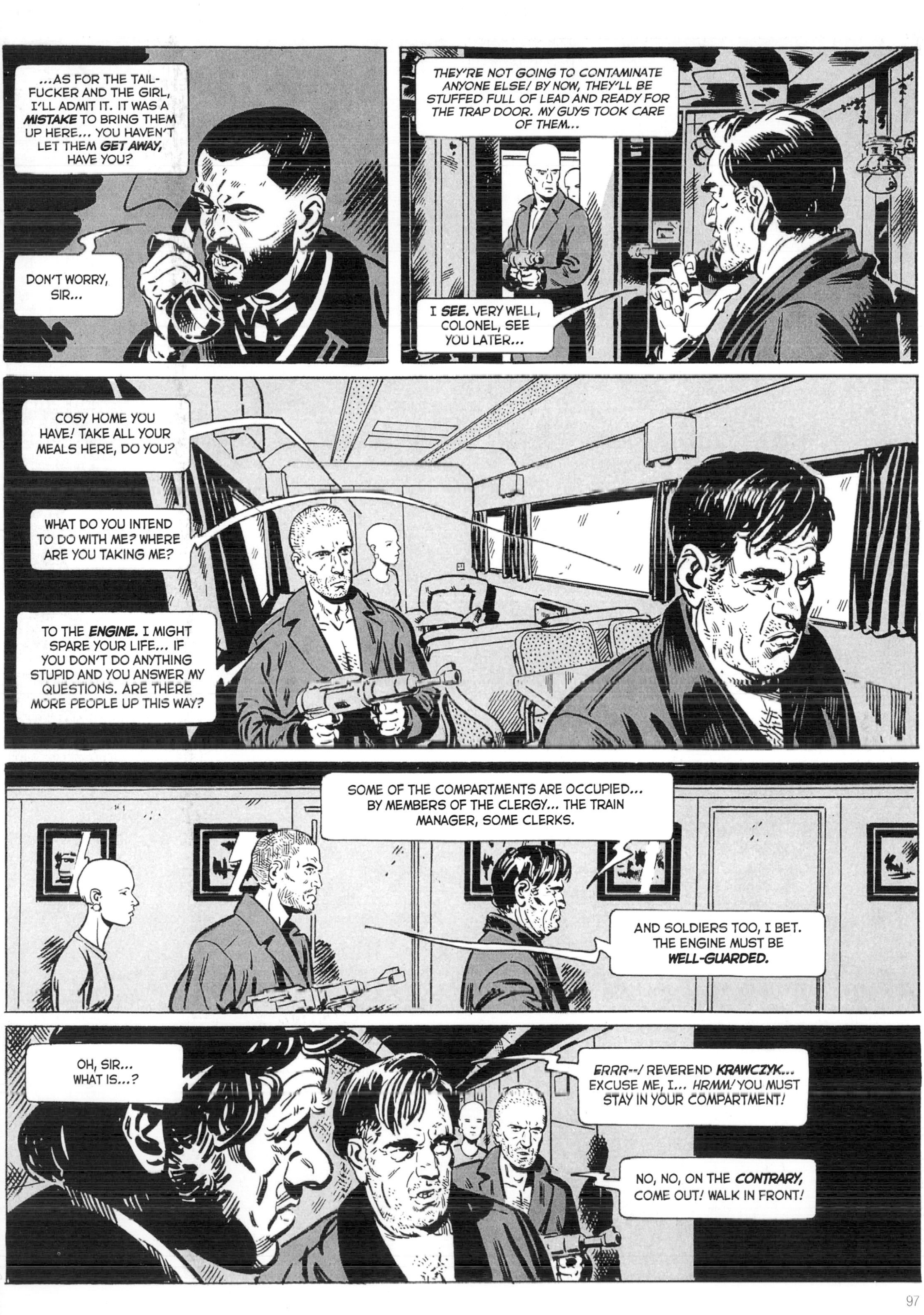
...AS FOR THE TAIL-FUCKER AND THE GIRL, I'LL ADMIT IT. IT WAS A MISTAKE TO BRING THEM UP HERE... YOU HAVEN'T LET THEM GET AWAY, HAVE YOU?
DON'T WORRY, SIR...
THEY'RE NOT GOING TO CONTAMINATE ANYONE ELSE! BY NOW, THEY'LL BE STUFFED FULL OF LEAD AND READY FOR THE TRAP DOOR. MY GUYS TOOK CARE OF THEM...
I SEE. VERY WELL, COLONEL, SEE YOU LATER...
COSY HOME YOU HAVE! TAKE ALL YOUR MEALS HERE, DO YOU?
WHAT DO YOU INTEND TO DO WITH ME? WHERE ARE YOU TAKING ME?
TO THE ENGINE. I MIGHT SPARE YOUR LIFE... IF YOU DON'T DO ANYTHING STUPID AND YOU ANSWER MY QUESTIONS. ARE THERE MORE PEOPLE UP THIS WAY?
SOME OF THE COMPARTMENTS ARE OCCUPIED... BY MEMBERS OF THE CLERGY... THE TRAIN MANAGER, SOME CLERKS.
AND SOLDIERS TOO, I BET. THE ENGINE MUST BE WELL-GUARDED.
OH, SIR... WHAT IS...?
ERRR--! REVEREND KRAWCZYK... EXCUSE ME, I... HRMM! YOU MUST STAY IN YOUR COMPARTMENT!
NO, NO, ON THE CONTRARY, COME OUT! WALK IN FRONT!

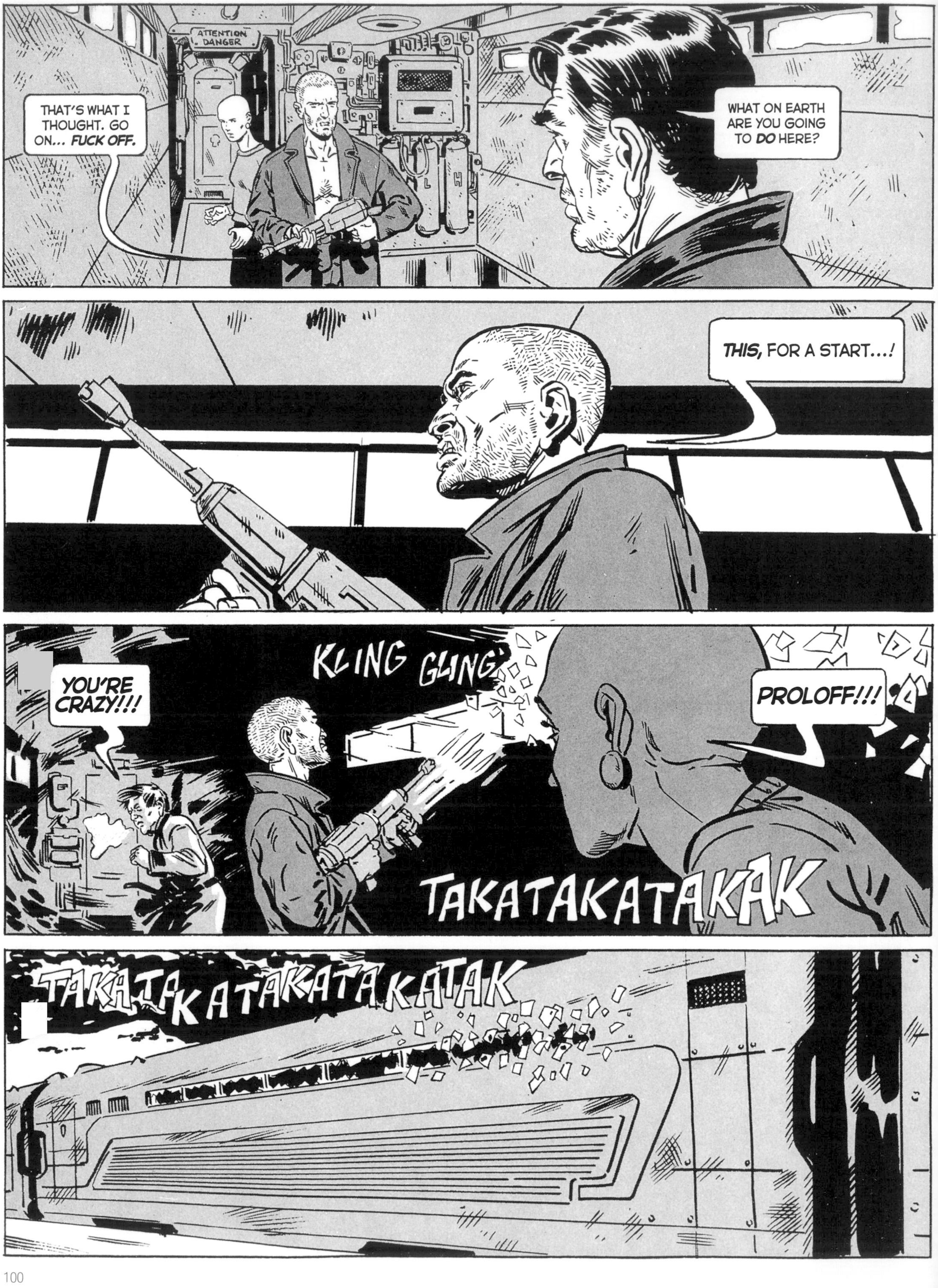
ATTENTION DANGER
WHAT ON EARTH ARE YOU GOING TO DO HERE?
THAT'S WHAT I THOUGHT. GO ON... FUCK OFF.
THIS, FOR A START...!
KLING GLING
YOU'RE CRAZY!!!
PROLOFF!!!
TAKATAKATAKAK
TAKATAKATAKATAKATAK

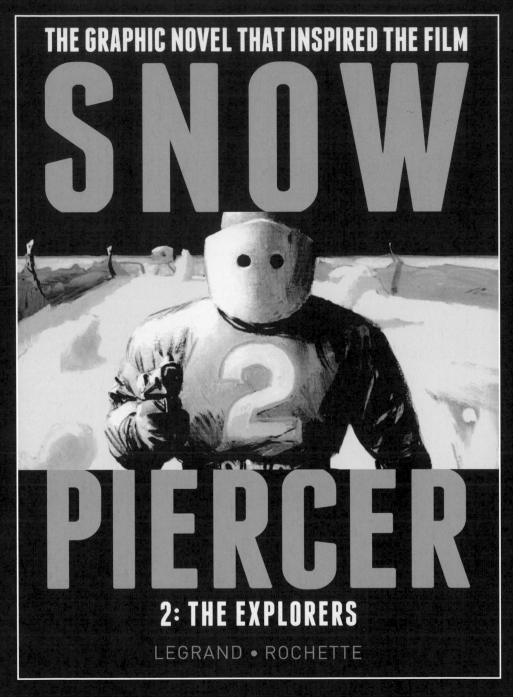

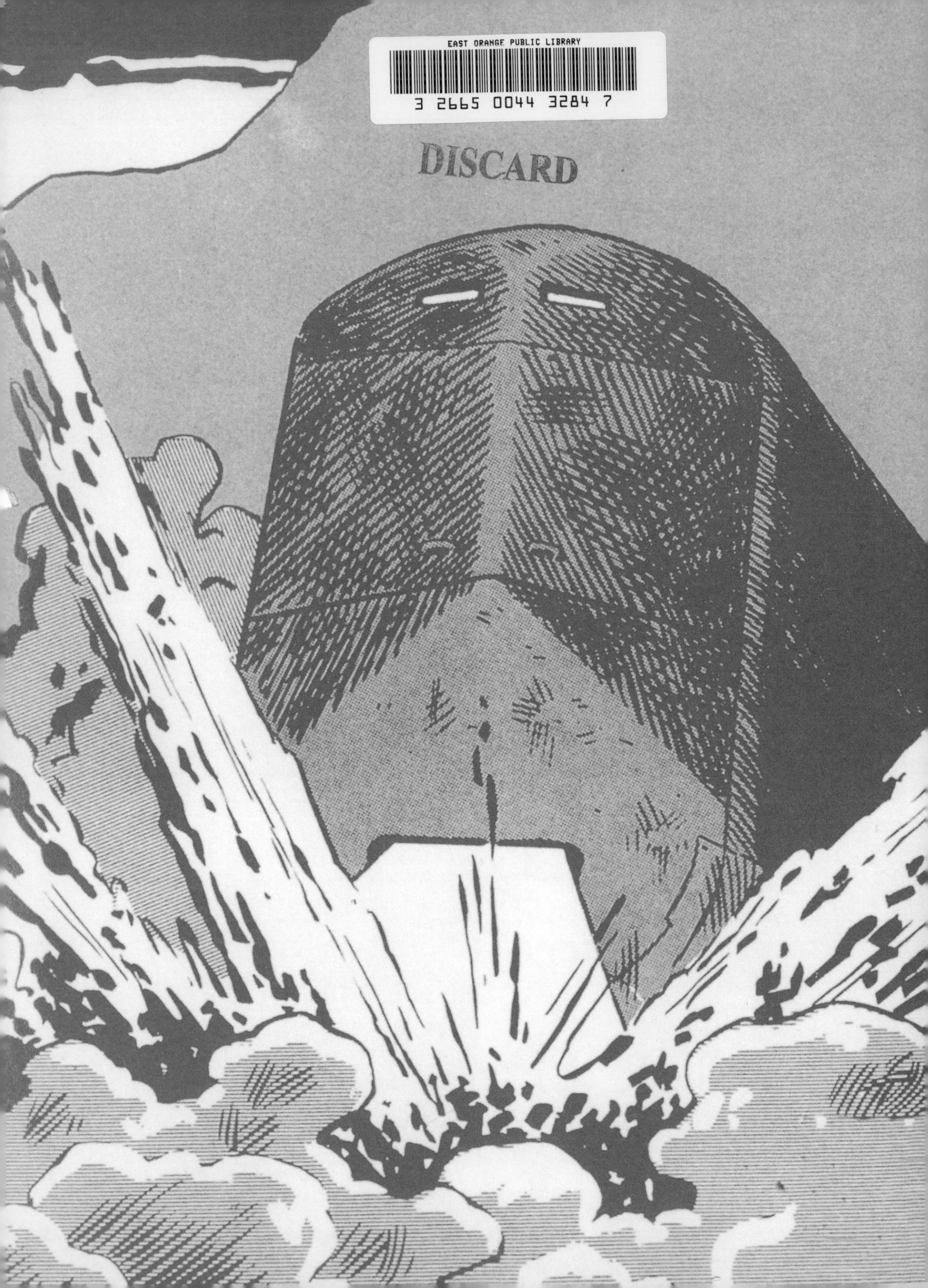